On Voice

On Voice

Speech, Song, Silence: Human and Divine

VICTORIA JOHNSON

DARTON · LONGMAN + TODD

First published in 2024 by
Darton, Longman and Todd Ltd
Unit 1, The Exchange
6 Scarbrook Road
Croydon CR0 1UH

978-1-913657-98-7

A catalogue record for this book is available from the British Library.

Printed and bound in Great Britain by Bell & Bain, Glasgow

Soli Deo Gloria

Contents

Acknowledgements

With thanks to all those who through encouragement and conversation have helped me find my own voice through this experience of writing. First and foremost, my family. Thanks to colleagues from York Minster, the Choristers, Choral Scholars, Vicars Choral, and Cathedral Musicians, Ben Morris and Robert Sharpe. It has been a joy to make music with them day by day. Thank you to the generous and welcoming communities of Virginia Theological Seminary, Merton College, Oxford and the collective minds of the Littlemore Group. Thank you to these wise and generous people as well: Rachel Mann, David Moloney, Sharon Jones, Anne Richards, Jennifer Beaumont, Rebecca Applin, Tim Stevens, Katy Cunliffe, Maggie McLean, Catriona Cumming, Hilary Barber, Ian McVeety, Christa McKittrick, Victoria Avery, Ben Liberatore, Andrew Scott, Carol Harrison, Jessica Martin, Katherine Sonderegger, and to all those people who have shared music and song with me since I first had a voice to sing with.

Foreword

G od speaks and it is the making of the world. His voice is no sounding thunder or a clanging cymbal. The voice of God calls the universe into being and sustains it. It is also the sound of pure silence, and the cry of a baby on that most holy night in Bethlehem; it is the agony of a man tortured on the Cross, and the voice of the One who calls us by name in the Garden of Reconciliation and in all those countless places where we long for forgiveness. Somehow, wonderfully, surprisingly and delightfully we his creatures – with our genius for getting it wrong – are invited to respond to these inflexions of grace with praise, thanksgiving and prayer. We are called to sing.

One of the reasons I adore Vicky Johnson's book is the depth of attention she gives to the dynamic interplay between the divine and human voice. Dare I say it, her attention thereby yields not only theological insight, but poetic and human insight too; she does not shy away from vulnerability. When Vicky says, 'I open my mouth and in a sense I'm in the hands of God. It's like leaping into the unknown, a flight of faith', she reminds me of the wondrous precariousness, the tenderness, of 'voice' in its many horizons. We tremble in the face of God, but the One in whose company we are in awe is no hectoring demagogue seeking to impress or repress; our God silences us both with the abundance of his silence and the exquisiteness of his song. In silence, ironically, often we find our truest voices.

As Vicky's commissioning editor, I have had the privilege of accompanying her from the first germ of the idea behind this book through to its final manuscript. What gripped me from the outset was her preparedness to range far and wide, drawing on her scientific training as well as her skills as a musician. Yes, this book includes almost forensic reflections on her experience as 'first singer' or Precentor in a major Cathedral – there is, then, appropriate autobiography – but Vicky has valuable things to say about voice, technology, and that most pressing, emergent subject, A.I.. I sense her insights in that area will only gather significance over time.

Of the many fine chapters in this book, however, I especially adore Vicky's meditation on the language and voice of bells. That great gentleman-detective and lay theologian Lord Peter Wimsey reminds us in Dorothy Sayers's *The Nine Tailors*, 'Bells are like cats and mirrors—they're always queer, and it doesn't do to think too much about them.' Certainly, Vicky treats with this inherent strangeness. However, by daring to think deeply about bells she also reveals that they hold an exquisite music of God which draws us deeper into the mystery of Church, Land, Nation, and that which actually abides. Bells may, indeed, be the voice of the Church.

I did not know I needed this book until Vicky wrote it. For me, that's high praise. Like all especially valuable books, *On Voice* foregrounds and reframes ideas in expansive ways; insofar as I had ideas about the theology of voice prior to reading Vicky's manuscript they were nascent and half-developed. This book is full of 'now I understand' moments. It shows us that whenever we think 'voice' is obvious and uninteresting it is mysterious and fascinating; it reveals that in the seeming ephemeral, passing nature of voice there is something timeless and essential; it indicates that particular voices tend towards something greater, even towards the Divine. I think this book will likely draw a reader closer to the Divine; it will definitely make her long to sing.

THE VEN. DR RACHEL MANN
Feast of the Naming and Circumcision of Christ 2024

Introduction
She who sings first

Tune me, O Lord, into one harmony
With Thee, one full responsive vibrant chord
Unto Thy praise all love and melody,
Tune me, O Lord.
Christina Rossetti

'm always nervous when I speak or sing in church. Always. The nerves never completely disappear, and I'd be worried if they did. The feeling of inadequacy never goes away. It's still a massive thing even though I do it pretty much every day. When I step up into a stall or into a pulpit, I need to focus and try to control my pounding heart and quell the rush of adrenalin coursing through my veins. Before I even open my mouth, I'm channelling every sinew of my body for this singular purpose. I need to be aligned within myself and to the task ahead of me. My ears are alert, my eyes scanning the words and notes in front of me, speaking them first silently in my head and then a deep breath.

I open my mouth and in a sense I'm in the hands of God. It's like leaping into the unknown, a flight of faith. This isn't just public speaking, it's speaking or singing between heaven and earth, making sound into a liminal space, and carving out a prayer that reaches from the material to the things which are above. Holding a space with your voice, gathering a community with your voice, using your voice to speak to the creator of the universe or sing in praise of that creator, takes considerable guts. It also takes some muscle, the concerted effort of flesh and blood, mind, body, and spirit, to produce something as ephemeral as the dew in the morning that goes early away, something as fragile as blossom shaken from the tree by the whisper of the wind, something as transiently beautiful as the flower that fades. It is there and then it is gone. Evaporated.

I can't compete, either by stature or significance, with the magnificent building in which I work, it rules me, and I am overawed by it. I must respect the holy boards I tread and become part of that fabric of prayer and praise, working with the grain of the wood, stone and glass towards the same end; only the biggest ecclesiastical ego would try and win over a space like this. This sacred space always wins. It has its own identity, and indeed its own voice. In some respects, the public work of prayer that I offer is all down to my voice and how it works in this laboratory of worship: its tone, its timbre and rhythm, its direction and pitch, its purpose and its clarity. How words sound, matters here. Voices sound different in this space. When the sun bursts through the stained glass and the air is bright and cold, a voice might become invigorated and lively, when the night draws in and candles flicker, the voice carries the numinous and mystical, when the crowds jostle and the nave is full, the space requires the voice to take on the role of a captain, clear, directive and confident and on a rare occasion the voice needs to have the comedic timing and cadence of a stand-up comedian.

The role I inhabit is called *Precentor*. It literally means *'the one who sings first'*. It's an ancient office which reaches back into the earliest worship of the Hebrew people and was then translated into the life of the early church. Historically, the role of such a cantor was bestowed with the stewardship of worship, and the integration of liturgical time and its eternal promise, alongside more temporal concerns. In a detailed study of the role of cantors during the Medieval period, liturgical time and the reality of the word made incarnate were both 'voiced' through the elements of the liturgy: 'the psalmody, readings from the Old and New Testaments and the lives of the Saints'.[1] The past was woven into the present through remembering, re-enactment and the re-iteration and re-voicing of received truths. Through this cycle of prayer and praise, symbol and sacrament, the future was made through a living tradition, a moving place of continuity and change, a place of history and possibility; this tradition was articulated through the voices of those charged with its stewardship and its development, and it was not only spoken, it was also sung.

In some ways I do what precentors or cantors have always done, leading worship, intoning, praying, singing, ensuring the dignity of worship is maintained and overseeing the musical and liturgical life of a cathedral. I also collate and shape liturgical time and align it to the time we inhabit in the twenty-first century, orchestrating what the church and the world may need to hear or attend to in order to proclaim the gospel afresh, whilst worshipping the God who is the same, yesterday, today and forever. There is also quite a lot that is not directly related to music or prayer as the modern-day cathedral requires good governance and financial management, long-term strategic vision and effective day to day running. But beneath the heritage, the tourists, the concerts, exhibitions and events, there is a sense in which I am still inhabiting a rather ancient position. The role of Precentor here dates back to 1093 and as the

---

[1] *Medieval Cantors and Their Craft. Music, Liturgy and the Shaping Of History, 800-1500*, edited by Katie Ann-Marie Bugyis, A. B. Kraebel and Margot E. Fassler (University of York, York Medieval Press, 2017).

centuries roll onwards from there, the names of my seventy-five predecessors are carved into the wooden board at the back of the Cathedral. My name now appears on this panel, the first woman in a history of nearly a thousand years. My voice is now being folded into the aural history of this place, one voice among many who have led prayers here, but nevertheless a new voice which has only relatively recently been given permission to sing or speak in significant spaces like this.

Shaping time through song

In York, there is a beautiful tradition of singing what we call an 'aisle prayer' before and after a choral service. Each night, just before the service of Evensong, we stand in the quire aisle, out of sight, and sing these prayers. These are, in essence, vestry prayers, readying the hearts and minds of those who lead worship, both choir and clergy. There is a different prayer for each day taking us through a kind of liturgical week from the Ascension on Thursdays to Easter on Sundays. Every Friday is an echo of Good Friday, every Saturday anticipates the resurrection and reminds us that through Christ we are drawn from death to life. The prayer for Sunday reminds us that what we offer through worship is a service and a sacrifice to God Almighty. These prayers literally set the tone for what is to come and conclude what has been offered. They are cantored in unison, on one single note. All voices, high and low singing as one voice, without flourish or adornment, book-ending our praise with prayers elevated by being sung.

As the name suggests, in the side-aisle and from a distance, I sing '*Thou art worthy at all times to be hymned with holy voices, Son of God, giver of life*', words drawn from one of the first Christian hymns, the *Phos Hilaron*. The choir respond, '*Therefore the world glorifies thee*'. The hymn was written in the first century of the church and accompanied lamp-lighting at the end of the day as the church gathered for worship. As night drew in, those early Christians raised their voices along with the whole of the created order, a myriad of voices offered in praise.

We pray as we sing, we sing as we pray, and we petition that we be moulded into the right frame of mind to lead worship as an offering on behalf of all things that give glory to God. In many other contexts similar prayers are *said* before or after worship, but what difference does it make if they are sung? To sing a prayer seems to solemnify the offering, it somehow unifies the hearts of those who pray with a seriousness and a stillness. Singing a prayer seems to weave together all that we are in an offering of praise. To sing a prayer is to embody a prayer and let that prayer shape you and melt into your bones and breathe life into your flesh. I can't describe how focussing it is to sing a prayer like this, it sharpens us, it holds us back from rushing, it takes away pride, it tunes us for worship. These holy voices, our voices, in that moment have been set aside for this purpose alone and yet this way of praying is a means of connection and of relationship. We are bound together with one another through every ounce of our being, and we are bound to our calling by, through and for God. We pray that what we sing with our lips, we believe in our hearts, and what we believe in our hearts we practise in our lives.

Once the prayer in the aisle has been offered worship begins and we process into the quire two by two in that quintessentially Anglican way, all cassocks and surplices and gently gliding feet. The organist carefully navigates a transition from the A440 where I began into the key of the opening responses and lands on a chord from which I can leap off into those ancient words from Psalm 51: 'O Lord open thou our lips', and the choir sing back: 'and our *mouth shall show forth thy praise'*. At its very best, Anglican worship in this tradition is like a seamless robe and its careful orchestration shapes time and space, a kind of immersive re-enactment of the worship of the heavenly hosts, which is the fulfilment of our praise, and I would suggest, is always sung.

For me singing is always prayer. Sidestepping the issue of whether it was or was not St Augustine who wrote *'to Sing is to pray twice'*, for me this holds true. Singing is the most fulfilled way that I pray, the most complete. It represents an expression of my faith, a total embodiment of prayer, a tuning of my whole body for praise. Sometimes I think that singing is one of the few things that I do that requires one hundred and ten percent of me; though a mathematical impossibility, it requires all that I am and somehow more. There is no room, when singing, to be thinking of something else. It is impossible to let your mind wander because the effort is consuming your body, mind, and spirit to such an extent that it takes you away from yourself through a singular and all-consuming purpose. There are some occasions, as I have been singing the responses at Evensong, or whilst intoning a collect, or singing a gospel, when it feels as if I have lost myself and been so fully immersed in the words of the prayer and the music that carries it, that I have no memory of what I have just done, it's rather like a holy absence. When these moments are over and the music stops, I suddenly wake up. It's as if I am using a different part of my consciousness and singing seems to take me there.

On being heard

Though I am usually focussed enough to direct my singing as a prayer towards God, I never expect people to listen uncritically, because for all this is prayer, in the real world it is also performance. Whatever I sing or speak is often judged. I feel I need to earn the ears of those who are listening and that goes for preaching too, another form of vocal proclamation which I am called to do. In this context, speech and song need to be heard. Diction and clarity are vital. As the hymn says, how will they know, if they have never heard? Some of my predecessors used their speaking voice in a very particular way. There are still those who remember what was like to attend worship without sound reinforcement technology. How were voices projected in a space like this before the microphone? Clergy developed a means of throwing their voice, whether through breath-control or sometimes through speaking with a chant-like quality: a 'singsong' voice, which was more able to carry words through the air. Over time, this may have evolved into that phenomenon commonly known as the 'parsonical voice', that slightly condescending and slightly nasal voice beloved by clerics of yore and still part of Anglicanism's soundscape. The parody vicar voiced by Alan Bennet in his 1964 sketch, 'The Sermon' (or 'Take a pew'), exemplifies this affectation very clearly. To be ribbed so mercilessly by a comedic genius, suggested that the parsonical voice was already a long-standing Anglican 'trope'. In 1927, a short article in an Australian Newspaper,[2] reported on a Church Assembly Meeting in London, where a Mr Charles Harris requested that Archbishops and Bishops ensure that those training for ordination received voice production lessons. Any interference with the natural voice was condemned and the 'Oxford affectation' as it was called, a way of sounding vowels amongst largely Oxford clergy, was particularly critiqued.

[2] The *Western Argus* was published in Kalgoorlie, Western Australia, between 1894 and 1938. The article cited was published on Tuesday 25 January 1927, illustrating that the clerical voice was a concern even for the English speaking Anglican Church on the other side of the world as well as the Church of England.

In 1937, Basil Maine, organist and music critic, petitioned for these clerical tones to be banned from the airwaves, being as detrimental to good speaking as crooning was said to be to good singing. He said the broadcasting corporation should not tolerate it, even if it meant barring prominent men from delivering their sermons on the radio. He preferred an announcer to read the sermon and said that even if the cleric lulled themselves into a pseudo-reverent state of mind, the listeners would not be so deceived.[3] It seems that he was longing for a sonic authenticity rather than an affected performance. People can discern a great deal from the 'tone' of your voice. I am often in agreement with Basil Maine and one of my deepest fears is that I sound too much like a cleric. I pray daily that I may never lull myself into a pseudo-reverent state of mind and I must be careful how I use my voice to lead prayer.

Those who listen need to have faith in the voices of those who lead worship. I feel that people need to have faith in my voice because my voice must somehow carry the prayers of others as well as my own, it cannot be a distraction from prayer. My voice must have a transparency that leaves space for others to sing through their imagination and let the words of my prayers become theirs. My speaking voice has to bear the voices of others and shepherd them; I have to somehow allow others to feel as though they are speaking through me and with me to God. My voice must be both intimate and authoritative, earthy and genuine and yet leading others to the transcendent. None of this is about accent or pitch or impediment, some of the most beautiful voices I know are drenched with the accent of their place,

---

[3]   'CLERICAL VOICE.' (1937, January 22). *Advocate (Burnie, Tas. : 1890 - 1954)*, p. 1. Retrieved 21 December 2021, from http://nla.gov.au/nla.news-article68457301

or the cracks of their physicality, the voice is more than the effects of our geography and our biology, it is more profound and more fundamental than that. Our voice both reveals us and betrays us. Our voice represents a layering upon layer of who we are: our roots, our culture, our being, our vocation, our desires and our dreams, our faith. The voice is a window into the soul and an outward and visible sound of the heart.

In addition to the sheer terror of speaking publicly and being the voice that breaks open worship, there is also an additional weight of history laid upon my shoulders; the history of people like me *not* being permitted to speak or sing in church over millennia. These days I am not *that* unusual. I am just a woman, and I have grown up in an era during which women have found their voice in the liturgical life of the church despite centuries of silencing. But this is still a relatively recent phenomenon, and the critical ears are still there as well as the waspish words. I have been relatively unscathed by such comments, but I have had them: *I can't get used to a female voice singing those responses*, said one, *it doesn't seem right.* I have heard of other female clergy being condemned as having a voice which is *not loud enough* or speaking with a *high pitched voice* or a *childish voice*.

For some reason, the particularity of my sex is something that I have tried to generally play down in my ministry, especially when I was first ordained. A question might be raised as to why I have felt the need to somehow silence myself. *I am just doing the job*, I would often say. I just happen to sing exactly an octave sharp. *I am just a priest*, I would say, doing my job to the best of my ability. But time and time again, I can be surprised by the newness of the sound of my voice when speaking or singing in worship and I'm awestruck at what my voice is permitted and able to carry. I am not just doing a job or even stepping into a role. I have been called by God to this ministry, to pray, to preach, to sing and I have been called as

I am in all my imperfect and particular embodiment, in all of my uniqueness. I am called just as I am, with my own voice, just as we are all called.

I have cherished those moments when I speak the words of Christ during worship, when I sing the gospel as 'evangelist' in Holy Week or when I preach using my own words. I treasure the public reading of scripture, and particularly the gospels when my voice sounds the voice of Christ or when I sing the Eucharistic prayer. I am sometimes caught up short when I realise that I may be the first female voice to sing or speak these words in this context, bearing ancient prayers and liturgies to the world as if they are being born again, giving them a new voice. And yet, I know that along with the privilege I have of being heard and the joy I experience in leading worship, there are many other voices that are still silenced, voices not heard.

One of the joys of my role is inviting unheard voices to read scripture and be heard in public. The sounding of the voice of God, and the sounding of the voice of Christ mediated by the diversity of the church is a reminder that these words are for everyone to speak, God's voice is in all of us, in Christ we are one voice, made of many voices. There is still much work to do in ensuring those who are chosen to speak and sing in church are truly representing the wonderful diversity of the people of God in all their embodied particularity and uniqueness, and then there is even more work to do in challenging the patriarchies, principalities and powers of the church to actually listen to them when they do.

When singing stopped

My voice, which I do consider a precious gift, is thankfully fairly robust. A life of singing has trained these muscles to sing through coughs, colds, tiredness, and utter exhaustion

- if you can get through Beethoven's *Missa Solemnis*, you can surely get through anything? Just the once have I lost my voice completely. Over the course of a busy Christmas in the parish I could feel my voice ebbing away, urging me to stop, it was almost crying out in pain. There were just too many carols (and the associated descants), too many services, too many phone-calls, too many assemblies, too much altogether. Then on the twenty-seventh of December after taking an ambitious Boxing Day wedding, I was literally silenced. Though this is an obvious occupational hazard in professions like mine, it was a terrifying few weeks when my whole life seemed as if it was crumbling into pieces. If your voice is your work, your life, and your vocation, what happens when it's gone or when it has been taken away? I was genuinely worried I might never be able to sing again. My voice was brought back to life by antibiotics, honey and complete physical rest. I vowed to take much better care of it from that day onwards, which ultimately meant being careful with my words and taking much more care of myself in the throng and press of priestly ministry.

My own experience of losing my voice gave me the briefest insight into the many ways in which our voices are given and taken away. Since then, I have always been attentive to the fragility and power of the human voice. I have noted the times in scripture when a voice is lost, and someone becomes silent. I have noted the moments when someone believes their voice to be insufficient for some commission and God somehow gives them a voice to do the job. I listen to the stories of those around me who have endured chemotherapy, whose voice has been weakened or lost, whose voice box, or larynx has been surgically removed. I hear the bewilderment of those whose voices have changed or are changing and how our identity is closely entwined with our voice. I reflect with those whose voices have been silenced by oppression, grief or anxiety and I have known the pain at being unable to use my voice in song. I wonder in amazement at the power of human beings to recognise one another through voice alone, and the small miracle of children being calmed by the voice of a parent. I know that the baby in the womb can hear the voice of their mother and I have been the voice at a bedside reading Psalm 23 as someone takes their final breath and drifts towards a greater light. I have been the voice that releases someone from their sins and commends a soul to eternity.

My temporary and singular experience of voice loss was as nothing when compared to the time when everyone stopped singing. A virus we are all familiar with spread around the world through aerosols and through the breath, and the more people spoke the more it multiplied. It was carried on planes and journeyed across oceans, it spread from family to family, appearing both as a lethal and life limiting illness and as nothing more than a chesty cough. Intangible and uncontrollable, coronavirus put a stop to every kind of social gathering and atomised the voice of humanity. The human family was no longer a chorus of creation, but became a collection of isolated voices, many mediated via a screen, many left unheard. The noise of humanity was quietened down and as we were shut up, the sound of nature became more pronounced. We could hear the birds singing again as they took up our song.

As well as the profound effects on life in general, the virus obliterated artistic and cultural communities and its long-term effects are likely to be felt for years, we are still accommodating trauma. In my world, somewhere between the third and fourth Sunday of Lent, choirs and choral societies ground to a halt, orchestras disbanded, pubs and restaurants closed. There was no communal eating, drinking or being merry. The whole earth was being called into what seemed like penitential season of silence, solitude and restraint. Churches were locked and even the clergy were banned from entering. Worshipping communities of faith were ripped violently from the music and liturgies that had sustained them over centuries – a modern day exile. The thought of celebrating Easter without music was devastating, we could not even sing Alleluia together. I felt like something precious had been taken away. Corporate hymn singing was banned, church and cathedral choirs limped on by rehearsing online, and some even collected their disembodied voices and re-membered their choirs through skilful multi-track wizardry. As the pandemic wore on, it became apparent that singing was considered a dangerous sport. With each easing of the restrictions, endless risk assessments were created to enable at first, just one single cantor, then three or four, then six voices to offer praises to God, all with masks or stood behind Perspex screens or standing at least two metres apart. It felt as if we were being deconstructed and the voice of the church was being fractured and silenced.

As the pandemic wore on, so incensed were the singers of the United Kingdom by their continued silencing, that a petition was instigated appealing for amateur choirs to be permitted to sing together again. The petition picked up tens of thousands of signatures of singers who had been silenced for months, whilst thousands of football fans were permitted to sing loudly and lugubriously in close proximity. And of course, unbeknownst to everyone, there were parties being held in government offices that ran late into the night with singing, dancing, drinking and merriment.

At one point during the summer of that first lockdown, the only voice which could adorn worship musically was mine. My song was vicarious. I, as Cantor, stood at the West End of the largest Gothic Cathedral in Northern Europe and the Organist accompanied me from around fifty metres away. Somewhere in the arc that ran from one end of the building to the other, our music, expressed in the words of the Magnificat and the simplicity of plainsong, met in the air, and softened the silence that we were being conditioned into accepting, comforting the hearts of those who were able to leave the house. What did this awful year through which we journeyed, teach us about the corporate voice of the church as we laid down our instruments as if in strange land?

Vocation

Beyond motherese and nursery rhymes, my earliest memories of singing, place me in the back of a car singing along with my dad to Simon and Garfunkel or The Carpenters. This was uninhibited singing for singing's sake. Not a performance, not for any purpose, not for any educative reason. This was singing for the joy of it, immersed in close harmonies, this parent and child were singing together. Dad would take Simon, I'd take Garfunkel; I'd take Karen, he'd take Richard. Sometimes he'd swap cassettes and we'd get a blast of Handel's Messiah, a piece which has cropped up again and again at significant moments in my life, but it all started with a cassette in a car, windows open, singing at the top of our voices in the brown Austin Allegro as it trundled along coastal roads. Pure bliss.

There was no professional musical line in my family, neither a religious one. Perhaps somewhere in the long distant family history there was a local preacher somewhere or a great-great-grandmother who played a barrel organ, but otherwise, mine was an unremarkable musical childhood. I remember songs at school during assembly, I recall particularly 'Lily the Pink' to whom we'd drink, - a strange song for children to be singing - and 'Nelly the Elephant'. I still know all the words. I remember the mournful 'Think of a world without any flowers' and I remember my teacher sat on her desk playing guitar and teaching us to sing 'Peace is flowing like a river' with accompanying actions. As I reflect now on those anonymously written words and that anonymously written music, I give thanks for that simple little melody which is engraved on my heart, and words so simple that a child can carry them through life: let the mighty love of God flow through me, live through me, speak through me.

I also remember calmly filing into assemblies accompanied by the lyrical 'Cavatina' from the soundtrack to *The Deerhunter,* obviously the kind of music used to sedate lively children. I remember recorder club (for anyone unfamiliar, recorders were the ukuleles of the 1980s), and my favourite: 'Music and Movement' in the school hall when we were allowed to let rip and run around to Edvard Grieg's, 'In the Hall of the Mountain King' from the Peer Gynt Suite. There were choirs, wind bands and orchestras, and at home mine was a family where music and song were peppered through conversations and events, cut to my Granny singing 'Que sera, sera' or her rendering of 'Tiptoe Through the Tulips' as we ranged through the marigolds, daisies and gladioli in the garden; imagine singing along with the mice in *Bagpuss,* imagine kids in the back of a car laughing and singing 'Oh I do like to be beside the seaside'. Singing was just one expression of unbridled childhood joy, it had no purpose, it was anti-utilitarian, but it was leading me into a vocation to offer praise through song.

Then, in ways beyond my comprehension, this childhood musicality was somehow noticed and harnessed. In those days, music in school (and just an average and unremarkable state school at that) was valued and cherished. Arts and music education were taken for granted. For me, amid fractions, creative writing, and spelling tests, music was the place where I could be free. I remember suddenly having extra lessons, I didn't know why. From the recorder group, I seemed to graduate to violin lessons every Friday in the library, then the clarinet seemed to pop up from nowhere. I was lugging my instruments to school most days of the week, along with the cooking basket and PE kit. There was no 'music room' at home and no pushy tiger parenting making me practise. I think my parents were bemused as to where this was all coming from. My dad had strummed the guitar when he was younger and he could sing in tune, but otherwise his primary musical formation in the rural West Midlands was Black Sabbath and Deep Purple. If people have had no opportunity, how do you know if they are musical or not? Can everyone sing if given the chance? Surely this is a gift for everyone, not just those who can afford it?

Nevertheless, the music making in my life started to push at the predictable doors of class and privilege. My musical journey began because I had access to music through the school day, and that was a given. The cost of the instruments on which I played was subsidized, as were the lessons for a time. My parents had to scrimp and save to pay for private lessons as I clocked up the grades on three instruments. The school timetable and free school music lessons could only take me so far. I'm very grateful that they did, but even as a teenager I harboured a sense of guilt as it felt like my parents were wasting hard-earned money from their double shifts at Tesco and long days in a local authority works department to enable me to play Mozart's Clarinet Concerto. It was hard to balance the aesthetics and beauty of a musical education and the joy I gained from it, with the utilitarian necessities of life in general. Music, for a working-class family like mine, always felt like a luxury and sadly, a musical education has become even more of a luxury since, all too easily wiped from curriculums and considered as an almost frivolous optional extra. It's impossible not to reflect on musical pedagogy without straying into issues of access and diversity and without seeing music as something that only middle-class people can afford to do. This is still a challenge for the world of music. I'd often practise my instruments whilst watching the TV, or in the bedroom which I shared with my sister as she did her homework lying on the bed. My practice was always in fits and starts, erratic, and always being distracted by dogs, cats, little brothers, mum hoovering or shouting from the kitchen 'Tea's ready'.

At about the same time as I was discovering music at school, we kids got sent to church. Like little reverse apostles we were sent to retrieve the good news and bring it home. Mum and Dad didn't come with us, but they did send us off with some money for the collection, which we duly spent on sweets or ice-cream on the way home. As I look back, it was clear they were simply getting rid of us for a few hours on a Sunday morning. Who can blame them? But I think this is where things changed gear again and where the 'secular' music I was learning suddenly took on a new dimension and purpose.

After finding Sunday School dull, we were gently shepherded into the church choir. It was three for the price of one: me, my sister and my brother, a little slice of a *Von Trapp* cake, a trio of un-harnessed cherubic voices ripe for choral training and the strains of Samuel Sebastian Wesley. Without realising it, we were being enculturated into the totally predictable and prosaic 'choral-floral' tradition of middle-of-the-road Anglicanism that did what it said on the tin. This was the world of cassocks and surplices, crimped neck-ruffs, 'Carols for Choirs', processions, the Alternative Service Book; this was a culture of harvest suppers, baptisms, weddings and funerals, bell ringing, Choral Evensong and of course the obligatory jumble sale and summer fete. Everything was somehow familiar. It was like being enfolded into something that was well grounded and confident in its own identity, and that something also had its own sound. The soundscape of this kind of Anglicanism was comforting and predictable: the plagal cadences, the sursum corda, the hymnody, the organ bellowing and stirring souls to sing, the slow and deliberate reading of scripture, the rhythmical liturgical prayers and memorable and poetic words. I am sure that this soundscape is evident in my voice as I use it today, I carry with me the sonic imprints of my Christian formation.

Born to sing

When I started to sing in the church choir, aged about eight, girls were not permitted to sing in cathedrals, women had been effectively written out of the Anglican Choral tradition (or rather, they had never been let in), and at that time there were no women priests either. I was a parish chorister working hard towards blue and red medals for choral achievement and any ambitions to sing in a great cathedral had to be fulfilled by 'Come and Sing' events or diocesan festivals where 'proper' boy choristers paraded and processed in their perfectly starched ruffs and demonstrated to mere parish choristers like us, how good they were. They deigned to honour us with their presence. I'm sure that's not how they felt, but that's how it felt to me. Of course, it wasn't their fault, they were just part of the system, part of the 'elite' soundtrack of Anglicanism. Nevertheless, it felt, quite simply, unfair, and exclusive. Why was it that my voice (which worked in pretty much the same way and sounded just as nice, and to most ears sounded no different at all) wasn't good enough to praise God in a cathedral? Why was I not allowed to sing like them? It was unfathomable. I remember when my brother was about eight, there was a flurry of a possibility that he might have the potential to become a 'boy chorister' as there were voice trials at the local cathedral. My mum looked surprised, my sister was upset, and I was jealous. After about five minutes of earnest discussion and nodding sagely from all concerned, it was quickly decided we didn't want to send him away to something which felt like a medieval monastery for a superior education to sing a superior song; the whole enterprise, in those days, didn't feel like it was designed for people like us.

In the parish, we were nurtured by a skilled musician: the 'vicar's wife' who, whilst inhabiting some of the usual expectations of that role by making un-sugary cakes and chutneys, also happened to be a brilliant classically trained organist who could roll out a Bach Prelude or Widor's Toccata, without any trouble. In the choir vestry, week by week, egged on by her brilliance, I sang and I sang, unaware that what was being nurtured in me was a yearning to use my voice to praise God in speech and in song and in ways that were then well above my station. I was also unaware that I was imbibing the soundscape of Anglicanism and my voice was taking on the echoes and resonances of this tradition. The organs, the bells, the hymns, the choirs, the carols, I was being assimilated into the well-tempered and carefully measured pace and metre of the Church of England.

Music and song spilled over from my school day, and into my life as a whole. My instruments were drawn into worship, playing voluntaries before the service on the clarinet and playing along in parish musicals. This routine began to shape me, the rhythms of the church year were being planted in my soul, and the connection between music and faith got stronger and stronger. I was encouraged to read and lead prayers in church from the age of about ten, and I dutifully read scripture and began to understand how to be heard as a voice within worship and how to inhabit those words. I also remember being enraptured by the liturgy that I observed from my choir stall. As I looked on week by week and the priest spoke the words of the Eucharistic prayer *'Take, eat, this is my body given for you, do this in remembrance of me'*, I knew I wanted to say those words too, with my own voice. I had no concept of what this might mean. I had no concept that this wasn't even possible, but I did want to make those words my own, and speak them with my own lips. It was somewhere in this mix that my vocation to sing and my vocation to be a priest became entwined. I am a priest who sings, a singing priest, and for me, the two go together like a horse and carriage. Today, the heart of my vocation is found in singing and speaking the liturgy.

Of course, I was blissfully unaware of the ructions that were going on above my head at that time. What right thinking teenager would be that interested in the Church of England? I was too young and absorbed in school life to care much for the news reports showing protests outside General Synod and abuse being hurled at women who wanted to follow their vocation. I wasn't really affected by the opinions of 'prominent' Anglicans of the time, such as John Gummer and Ann Widdecombe who accused the Church of promoting political correctness above the very clear teachings of scripture. I wasn't really listening when the argument was made in public, at General Synod in 1992, that women could no more be ordained than could a pork pie. This language is rather astonishing and shocking even now, and the venom and anger against women who simply want to break bread as Christ commanded has not subsided. As this 'debate' ensued and agitated the conservative party at prayer, outside church politics, teenagers like me were singing along to Nirvana, 'Smells Like Teen Spirit', The Red Hot Chilli Peppers, 'Under the Bridge', and in secret (because it was soppy), 'I Will Always Love You' by Whitney Houston.

So, I just kept singing and while I was at it, took up the

piano and then the organ, via the nurture of the same Choir 'Mistress' (as she was then called). This involved turning pages and pulling out stops on her nod. By now, I had even less time to practise but I fumbled on and used to love going into a quiet church on my way home from sixth form college, to play about on the three manual Rushworth and Dreaper instrument, learning hymns and easy voluntaries and attempting to tri-furcate my brain to play right hand, left hand and pedals. It was a joy to experiment with sound in an empty church. I loved this instrument of many voices: flutes, diapasons, strings, brass, an orchestra at the tip of my fingers and an instrument which enabled the church to sing with colour and diversity.

How can I keep from singing?

When I was eventually ordained, I experienced a heart wrenching grief. In a sense, singing in a church choir had got me to this point. My love of singing with my own voice had given me confidence to enable others to sing with theirs, and I began directing choirs too - it seemed like a natural progression. But with ordination came a loss of this voice. I could no longer sing in a church choir or direct one. I was now leading the worship of the church and conducting its music in a different way, using my God-given voice in a different way. I was a little resentful at first. It felt like God was snatching away from me the very thing that had drawn me in. It did feel a bit cruel at the time. My first eucharist was an utterly joyful and unforgettable celebration, but as the choir sang Haydn's 'Little Organ Mass' which they had been practicing for weeks, there was just a little bit of me that was grieving as I stood at the altar silent in prayer as they joined their song with the song of the angels and archangels and the whole company of heaven.

This journey, begun in the back of car and on benches in a

fusty choir vestry, has led me to something of the zenith of the Anglican Choral Tradition. I work in a magnificent building with world-class musicians and incredible choristers (boys and girls, equal in every way) and a newly restored organ; an instrument of such epic proportions it can lift the voices of two thousand people in song. But all this sometimes feels very precarious, even here, as the church lurches from crisis to crisis and becomes more and more irrelevant to the masses who have found other distractions and a new soundtrack that gives meaning and purpose to their lives. It feels even more precarious as the stability of this tradition is gradually decimated and devalued. And yet, at certain times of year and on certain occasions, thousands upon thousands return to experience the evolving soundscape of Anglicanism. Every day, hundreds of people are drawn in to hear the voices of our choir singing Evensong. For many this is a first taste of something wonderful, a new sound world and a window into God.

My voice has somehow got me here and helped me respond to the one who calls. Every voice has a story. I now sing as part of my vocation and in a way, it's all come together in the end. Singing evensong day by day and singing the sursum corda of the mass and the preface that follows seem to me to be some of the most important things that I do. These are moments of connection, moments of transcendence beyond myself, moments when I become almost completely an instrument for God. I am a Priest who sings, and this singing makes sense of everything else. So, in the spirit of not taking this voice for granted, and neither taking for granted the gifts of speech, song, or silence, it seems appropriate and fitting to explore through this tradition, the history, meaning and theology of the voice, human and divine, and see what that exploration might unearth both for the church and for the world.

CHAPTER ONE

The Speech Act

The voice of the Lord on the waters;
the God of glory thunders;
the Lord on the immensity of waters;
The voice of the Lord full of power;
the voice of the Lord full of splendour.
Psalm 29

At the beginning of all things, God spoke. In the account of Creation in the Book of Genesis, it was God's voice that birthed the world into being. When God said, 'Let there be light', there was light. God speaks and things happen. Speech, light, action. The world is created by God's word, but it wasn't a written word like a set of instructions, it was a spoken word. Speaking is always a happening with God. What God *said* in that moment represented the beginning of all things. Before the beginning there was nothing that we can comprehend, but we know God was there ready to speak, the only voice of purest act. At first there was just a voice waiting to speak, a dialogue waiting to happen, gathering itself, and then there was the sound of a breath sweeping over the waters. From the breath came a sonic boom of cosmic proportions which created a new world of sound. The first words uttered 'Let there be light' brought illumination and life. What the voice of the Almighty sounded like in that moment we can never know, we can only hear this voice by seeing what it created, but it has been described as a voice that flashes flames of fire, as a voice that thunders, a voice of splendour, and in complete contrast, it has also been described as the sound of sheer silence.

Perhaps this voice which carved out day and night, earth and sky, was a musical voice, or rather music might be one of the ways we can comprehend its beauty and power, our nearest approximation of this music beyond music. From nothing, there came the sound of God before there were eyes to see or ears to hear, and that sound was a voice which combined a perfect harmony and melody, it was the origin of all music, sonorous and indeed glorious with its own rhythm and metre, vibrating and echoing, peeling open the vacuum until sound turned to light on the first day, making space and time. Like refracted light, this was sound expanded from a single point into a complete cacophony, sound exploding in every direction with limitless energy, making, shaping, creating, calling. This was the voice which spoke in the beginning and that voice was with God and that voice was God.

And it was this voice that set the sun, the moon, and the stars in the heavens, moulded dry land and brought vegetation and all green things to life. And then God spoke again, and life emerged, crawling and creeping over the earth, gliding through waters. It is worth stopping for a moment and reflecting on this voice which carries so much creative potential, a voice that builds up rather than destroying, a voice which plants. God's voice yielded life; it fashioned life; it was life. This life was rustling and whispering, the sound of sap was coursing through the veins of trees, leaves were unfurling, flowers blossoming and then fruits were bursting with sweetness; bubbling water was murmuring in streams and crashing waves were shouting upon the seashore; there was a chatter, clatter, flutter and buzz of insects and the trill and whistle of birds who made their own songs before music was ever written down. Before any human spoke, before there were any ears to hear, creation was already finding its voice, telling of God's handiwork; combining in symphonic force to make an earth-song of unimaginable beauty in a liturgy of unending praise, and the voice which it had been given was beginning to sound something like the voice of the one who created it, with its sound resonating throughout all the earth.

On the last day of creation, it became clear that the voice of God was not a lone voice: *Let us* make humankind in our own image, God said. This voice was in conversation, in dialogue with itself, the voice was already a community held together by a song of love. A divine council, a holy community of different voices singing together as one. The voice was a chorus from which other voices were born. Voice begets voice. God did not replicate a single voice in God's likeness but created another community of voices from the first; voices that were themselves capable of creating a community of many voices, multitudinous voices as numerous as the stars of heaven or as the grains of sand upon the seashore. Voices which would duet and entwine, one with another, weaving, embracing, a sweet conversation there in their little Eden. God could then speak with creation and creation could speak back to God.

Creation's Song

A musical articulation of this creative act is well and joyously made by Joseph Haydn, in his work 'The Creation' written between 1797 and 1798. In the recitatives and choruses, creation sings and proclaims the wondrous work of God, a vision influenced by the belief in the good ordering of the universe by divine wisdom. We are told, in a paraphrase of Psalm 19, that the heavens are telling the glory of God in worship and praise, and the word of God resounds across all lands, never unperceived, ever understood. God's voice is always heard and comprehended, there is no ambiguity; this sound permeates all things. The newly fledged humanity has ears to hear God's word and is delightfully obedient to it. The earth and everything in it are then given a voice which finds its purpose in giving praise to God the creator, it is almost like a jubilant beginning and a magnificent ending. Everything that is made is working towards this vocation, 'Sing the Lord, ye voices all' the final chorus belts out.

Haydn stops short of expressing in music the events of the fall; his oratorio doesn't quite get to Genesis, Chapter 3; perhaps after all the exuberance and joy of the creative act this was just too complicated and messy to express in feel-good eighteenth-century classical music. Haydn's perfect and unsullied Creation is kept in a pre-lapsarian state of grace. At the very end, there is just a passing reference in the libretto, noting that the happy pair, Adam and Eve, would still be happy if not for the false conceit of the serpent and their desire to know more than they should. This optimistic creation narrative is a window into a world of praise, unity, and concord just before it all went wrong or alternatively, a glimpse into a future beyond all time that is not yet ours, a premonition of the final doxology.

In the King James Bible, the third chapter of the Book of Genesis tells us that the man and the woman, after eating from the tree of knowledge of good and evil, heard the *voice of the Lord God walking in the garden.* Later translations replace the word 'voice' with the word 'sound' or 'noise'. The sound of God is one which enfolds the garden of creation but nevertheless the question remains: What does God sound like? As we ponder this question, we might begin to imagine the sound of God, the voice of God in the Garden on that day. God talking to Godself. God singing. God calling out to creation. They could hear God coming before they could ever see God and yet they hid from the voice of God, because they were naked, and they were afraid, guilty as sin. They tuned out as their concerns were occupied elsewhere; they had already switched to another channel.

This turn away from God's voice, this turn away from the call of God in the Garden of Eden, and the hiding from it, or rather the refusing to hear it, had been prompted by another voice: the snake, one of God's own creeping things. The serpent's words expose the first and greatest deception in all scripture when a persuasive and manipulative tone beguiles the woman to eat of the tree of the knowledge of life. This wasn't *do as I do*, this was very much *do as I say, listen to my voice.* The snake attempts to suggest to Eve that she had heard incorrectly, and that God's voice could not be trusted as true, *Did God really say that?* the snake asks Eve. Just as intriguing is how the serpent's voice was able to coax the ingénue to question her creator, to eat of the fruit of the tree of life and share that delight with her partner. The way the devil speaks is certainly something to ponder. In her musical morality play, *Ordo Virtutem*, the medieval mystic Hildegard of Bingen suggests that the devil cannot sing, the devil is devoid of any divine harmony, the devil grunts. If God is the summation of all music, if God is to be praised with 'heart and voice', [1] if God is to be praised in song, then it seems somehow musically correct that the devil should shout.

But in this biblical account of creation, the serpent's voice was beguiling and coercive. It was as familiar as it was strange; it was somehow recognisable. At the very same time it was slippery and undefinable, it was mesmerising and hypnotic. It was impossible not to listen to the serpents' voice, it was seductive, alluring, and irresistible. Upon the picking and eating of the fruit, the ears of Adam and Eve

[1] Hildegard of Bingen, *Scivias*, Book Three, Vision Thirteen (Paulist Press, New York, 1990), p. 529.

were no longer solely tuned in to the sound of God, and their preoccupation had turned inwards to themselves; they became enchanted by the sound of their own voice. And so, humanity's long travail begins, cursed with the proclivity to only hear themselves or those who sound like themselves to the detriment of the other and those who speak with a different voice.

In Medieval art, this scene in the Garden of Eden is often depicted with the serpent as having a human face, looking at Eve like a mirror, a depiction of the self, tempting her to eat.[2] If we think of this aurally, we could easily imagine the serpent as an able mimic. The sound of the serpent's voice was familiar to Eve, reflecting back her own voice or perhaps the voice of her beloved Adam. On another level it is possible to think of the serpent as speaking like a troubled and questioning conscience, an articulation of the self, the devil sat on the shoulder, whispering. But was there also something of the likeness of the sound of God's voice in those double-tongued words? Was the tricksy serpent mimicking not only Eve, but the voice the creator? After the transgression, there is the triple rebuke; the snake is cursed, the woman is given pain in childbearing, and the man is to toil for his food because very specifically, he listened to the voice of his wife.

From this muddle of innocence lost, confusion, deceit, and desire, it is still possible to imagine all this as a happy fault, whereby from that day onwards God yearns to have a voice recognised and heard by humanity, culminating in the voice of God being en-fleshed, and through that incarnation, salvation is offered for all. This is the beginning of a redemptive arc which resounds through history, and we

[2] See *The Temptation of Adam and Eve* by Tommaso Masolino da Panicale (1383-1447) or Giuliano Bugiardini's (1475-1554) representation of Adam and Eve.

can read it as such through the life of Christ, the second Adam. As the medieval fifteenth-century carol *Adam lay ybounden* offers, if the apple had not been taken, we would never have been able to sing with our own lips and from our own heart *'Deo gratias'*. The turn away enables the return, and the sin is ultimately redeemed by another song, in another garden when another woman recognises the voice of God, on the first day of a new creation.

From the moment the 'apple' was taken, the human being hasn't always known whose voice to listen to, and neither has the human being understood what their voices have been given for. Something happened before even the apple was picked, which resulted in Adam and Eve tuning out when God spoke; a proclivity defined not only as a turning away, but also as an inability or a refusal to recognise God's voice, the ultimate cause of our disobedience. This presents before us the tantalising possibility that, for human beings, God's voice is not necessarily pleasant to hear nor easy to recognise, and there are always going to be sounds far more enticing and voices that more easily distract or seduce. Time and time again, God pleads with the people to 'Listen to my voice', a constant divine command in scripture, but they, we, never quite grasp that our primary vocation is to listen to the voice of God. Through that listening we are called to use our voices in return to speak with God as a friend and offer praise, but again, we never quite grasp that vocation either.

At the very beginning of our holy scriptures, the sound story of our faith is introduced, we are introduced to the God who speaks, a creation which is spoken into being and the many complexities and nuances of voices, both divinely created and divine, and how they converse with one another. The first few chapters of Genesis represent pictorially that initial fragmentation and differentiation of voice from a single pure source, with a single pure purpose, into a multiplicity of voices. We also find there an articulation of, and deep yearning for, that which was from the beginning: the promise that one day the whole of creation in all its diversity and difference would sing together with one voice in unbridled harmony and find its purpose and vocation in worship alone.

Hildegard of Bingen held to this vision too. At the end of her work *Scivias*, she envisions a time when there will be a consummation of all things through praise and thanksgiving and jubilant song. It will be a return to everything as it was in beginning. The end of all time will be marked by the voices of a multitude lifting their sound on high in what she calls the 'Symphony of the Blessed'. The great reunion of all earthly and heavenly voices is the height of perfection, and ultimately the purpose for which we were all created.[3] John Mason in his wonderful hymn *'How shall I sing that Majesty?'* seems to come to the same conclusion. Here is a hymn of high exultation, a favourite of congregations and choirs, where the singer, a creature of praise, is contemplating how to respond to the God who presides over all things. The hymn articulates for the Christian soul their desire to sing and their realisation that their song may not be quite up to it, their voice may be too feeble and there may be a deficit in their praise. They petition and God responds. They appeal for light, a beam of brightness to illuminate them, and the sound of God comes to their ears. It is all sound and light. The lone singer is longing to be part of that heavenly choir, they are longing to be incorporated and embraced so that they can offer their praise in return and be one of the thousands who stand around the throne in unanimous chorus. In the end it seems there is a unification in praise and all things everywhere rejoice; the human voice is gathered up to sing with the heavenly host, where Alleluias resound

[3]   Ibid, p. 525.

forever.[4] The human voice returns to its origin and finds its true purpose.

Vox Dei

In the sixth and final book of his work, De Musica, St Augustine, reflects on the origins and constitution of the human voice and acknowledges that the human voice is, in all truth, a reflection or a living memory of the voice of God.[5] We are made in the image of God, the God who creates whole new worlds through speech and our human voice does, in some intangible and mystical way, represent something of the likeness of the sound of God's voice. Each human voice is a fragment of the divine. Each human voice is longing to find its true home in the sanctuary of God's heart, a home from home, our end and our beginning. In the popular imagination, the voice of God is deep and resonant and masculine, but this may testify to the limitations of our imagination rather than any true likeness. If God is both sound and light, then God's voice could be conceived as a sound made up of a spectrum, just as light is a spectrum of colour. God's voice is every voice of every frequency. God's voice is a rainbow voice which is made up of the sounds of red, orange, yellow, green, blue, indigo, violet.

In minute detail Augustine explores the beating heart of the human voice found in the undulation of verses, words, and iambs which, he suggests, is a rhythmic echo of the divine voice which created all things. Even in this deconstructed speech there is pitch, tone, cadence, pulse,

<hr/>

[4] In *Spiritual Songs, or Songs of Praise to Almighty God, upon Several Occasions; Penitential Cries,* John Mason and Thomas Shepherd (Leopold Classic Library, 1859). The hymn 'How Shall I sing that Majesty' is described in this volume as 'A General Song of Praise to Almighty God'.
[5] *St Augustine's De Musica*, A Synopsis by W. F. Jackson Knight, Book VI. The ascent from rhythm in sense to the immortal rhythm, which is in truth, p. 85.

and music. He teases out the voice into its constituent parts and finds in each a grain of the likeness of the voice of all voices. It seems that even in speech there is song and even when no words are uttered there is a voice. We are told that God created humankind in God's image, and we can think of that *Imago Dei* not only as something which is seen, but also something which is heard. We each have within us something of the likeness of the *sound of God*, or the *Vox Dei*. Every time we speak or sing or indeed hold silence, there is an echo of God's voice within our voice, a resonance of the divine.

Throughout the Hebrew Scriptures, God is known primarily by God's voice, from the Book of Deuteronomy we are told that the Lord spoke from the heart of the fire, 'you heard the sound of words but you saw no shape; there was only a voice.'[6] This voice speaks from beyond; it is a communication of God without intermediary. This is the voice that speaks to Adam and Eve. It is God's voice that commands the flood and speaks to Noah, it is God's voice that speaks from a burning bush to Moses; it is God's voice that speaks directly to Abraham, to the Kings, Saul, David, and Solomon. Then God speaks through the Prophets Isaiah, Jeremiah, and Ezekiel, putting his words in their mouth, the visions always accompanied by the voice and the prophets' constant refrain 'Hear, O Israel'. God is always seeking ways to speak with us, and we receive God's voice in varying ways, often unexpectedly and in the most unlikely people and places. God's voice is something we can be drawn towards or turn away from, something we can choose to hear or choose to ignore.

When Moses is stopped in his tracks whilst walking in the hill country tending the flock, he is assaulted by light and sound, vision and voice. He turns aside to see. The account of this revelation is made in Exodus, Chapter 3,

[6] Deuteronomy 4:12.

and in response, Gregory of Nyssa in his own account of the Life of Moses, offers that both his vision and his hearing are brightened by the rays of light and waves of sound. Eyes bright and 'his hearing illuminated'.[7] The burning bush is both a visionary and an auditory experience and from the fire, a voice from the light speaks to Moses. Again and again, we hear the voice, the daughter of a voice, speaking for God, but we never know what this voice sounds like and how it is made manifest upon the earth.

Through the fire and through this voice, God reveals the name: I am who I am, or I shall be whom I shall be, or I shall voice what I shall voice, and requests Moses to take that message to Pharaoh and liberate his people.[8] This should be a simple command and obey situation, how could anyone refuse? But there is a significant problem. Of all the people to call upon, Moses is slow of speech, he is not eloquent, and he doubts that anyone will listen to his voice as he is the first to admit he is an unskilled speaker. His well-founded reluctance kindles God's anger. The one who made the mouth could not be told who could speak and who could not speak. Moses' brother, Aaron, is commissioned as the mouthpiece or prophet of Moses, and to Aaron, Moses is like God, the one to whom he should listen. God will put his words in the mouth of Moses, and Aaron will speak them.

Why would God choose someone so inept to carry such an important message of liberation for the people of Israel? God chose a man whose voice was without authority or power and yet God could have chosen mighty kings and great orators as opposed to a man who might not be heard. Why would God choose such a convoluted strategy to share a message? The irony of Moses being chosen as the messenger

[7]   Gregory of Nyssa, *Life of Moses,* Introduction, Classics of Western Spirituality, (Paulist Press, 1978), p. 35.
[8]   Exodus 4:1-12.

to relay the word of God is not lost in this exploration of voice. There is in this moment an act of giving voice, a gift of a voice from the God who speaks. And this pattern repeats itself again and again in this story of the one true Voice: never the obvious choice, always the left-field. Never the loudmouth but always the lowly; a voice for the voiceless.

Centuries later, in the time of the judges, the revelation of God's voice is more discreet. There are no flashing fires or remarkable auditory experiences. We are told that the word of the Lord was rare in those days, and visions were not widespread. There was a silence and God didn't seem to be speaking at all, or rather, God was speaking all the time, but no one was listening. The people are not used to hearing God speak to them unmediated. This point is made narratively by the author of the first book of Samuel. It takes three attempts for Samuel to understand and recognise that it is God speaking to him in the temple and not the old man Eli. Once again, we see an ambiguity around recognising the divine voice and an uncertainty about who is speaking. [9]

The sound of our own voice

Human beings, in general, talk too much and as we have already discovered they rather like the sound of their own voice. The more humans speak, could it be the more our voices will echo something of the likeness of the sound of God's voice or, could it turn out to be exactly the opposite? The more humans speak, the more they think they will become like God. The more they speak, the less they hear. There is no better example of this fallacy, than the tale of the Tower of Babel. All we wanted was to be like God and build a tower up to the heights of heaven.[10]

[9]   1 Samuel, Chapter 3.
[10]   Genesis 11:1-9.

We all wanted to be the same, say the same, speak the same, sound the same and we thought this similitude would give us power. But God destroys the Tower of Babel and dissipates language and conformity to create instead (and once again) a world of diverse praise. This vision is emphasised on the day of Pentecost, as the Holy Spirit descends in tongues of fire and the disciples speak in many tongues; they all have different voices and speak in many languages, they do not say the same or sound the same. Uniformity seems to worry God. The Tower of Babel is toppled, and God usurps the human empire being built. It feels as if God does not want us all to sing with the same voice, we are not required to be assimilated, but the story of salvation does seem to be calling the many voices that God has created to join together in praise. The two are quite different.

When the voice of God dwells in the human body of Jesus Christ, this might cause us to pause and reflect on what this voice sounded like and what it effected in first century Palestine. Oh, to have heard that voice! In Christ, the voice of God is heard in temporality, birthed from flesh and blood. We know some of what this voice said, recorded in the Gospels, but we can only imagine what it sounded like and how the heavens poured out praise when, as a child, he screamed out with his first breath. Salvation history moves from a voice beyond to a voice embedded and embodied within creation itself. When God is made flesh, God is sounding within us, and that voice is then re-presented in music, poetry, literature and liturgy and the Christian imagination leads us to ponder the sound of Christ. This holy book of ours is not simply about the words on the page, it's about how they sound when they are spoken or sung, and the church is the sound that is created when these words are embodied by our voices in prayer and praise. It is also about the spaces between the words, like the gaps between the notes in a musical score. God is in the poetry, the prose and in the pregnant pause.

As a Christians, we are called to speak and sing the words of God and by embodying these words we find that the voice of God in Christ does not always have to be represented as one lower in register. The voice of God is too glorious and splendid to be trapped in the particularity of our humanity as we speak it in the liturgies of the church. As those who speak these words, we are picking up the fragments of this sound dispersed through all the earth, hoping that in the gathering we may all re-member this voice which was from the beginning.

Throughout the Christian tradition, the metaphor of light has been used to describe and understand something of the God known as Light of all light, but Hildegard and Augustine present the possibility that God is also Sound of all sound. Perhaps the sound which connects us most powerfully to the Almighty is when many voices are made one in a perfect harmony which leads ultimately to a perfect kind of stillness and silence. John Donne suggested much the same, speaking of an equal light and an equal music found in the ranges of eternity. It may be that in all of our speech and in all of our song we are somehow trying to attain that state of unity and concord with the one true voice, the Voice of all voices, the one who spoke us into being and orchestrates the music of the spheres. We are very used to thinking of Christians as being children of light, people of the book, but we forget that since the very beginning God's children have always, in fact, been people of the sound, people of the voice.

CHAPTER TWO

Vox Christi

How can a song signify a reality and how can
sound coming from a human mouth convey
the truth of the Spirit of God? [1]

The human voice is a remarkable instrument. A miracle
within a miracle. It begins in the womb of life as folds
of flesh are stretched and shaped and layered into a proto-
larynx to make the vocal cords of a tiny new being. Our
voice is begun at our inception and by the end of the first
trimester, just as our fingers are being printed with our
individuality, the instrument of our voice which is just as
unique, is also being made. The voice of the body which
cradles this tiny new being reverberates through blood and
water like an echo through space, to bring comfort through
its gentle murmuring, and the baby inside has ears enough
to hear the pitch and rhythm of their mother's voice to such
an extent that they begin to recognise the intonations of
language itself.

In the moment of her overshadowing, the glorious voice
which made the universe was being planted like a seed into
the earth of Mary, and the song which she would soon sing
was being formulated in her heart. When Mary sang the
song, we might imagine the child within her womb rejoicing
at the sound, absorbing those prophetic words in a moment
of the purest symbiosis. The song blossomed in Mary, her
soul magnified the Lord and her belly swelled. She sang of

[1] Joseph Gelineau, *Voices and Instruments in Christian Worship* (Burns
and Oates, 1964).

49

the proud being scattered and the powerful being brought down to earth, the rich being sent away and the lowly lifted up. This was the song she sang that day when she was at her most vulnerable and her most mighty, this was the song she continued to sing and this was the maternal soundscape that Christ would have heard as he waited, soon to be born.

In contrast to the prophets, Mary was not given the words to say or the song to sing from a voice beyond, the words of this song were already within her heart. She did not claim to speak with God's voice but it's clear that her words articulate the coming salvation that God was working through her. An unmarried teenage girl speaks in response to her calling, to bear the word of God to the world. This is the beginning of the project of liberation that Jesus' life will set in motion and the inauguration of the new kingdom he will proclaim. It may also caution the church against assuming it knows how the Christ will speak in the world today and whose voice God will choose to speak through. It seems as if Emmanuel, our God-with-us, will always choose to speak through the humble, the lowly, the little, the poor, the weak, the forgotten and the excluded, but will we have the ears to hear their song? The Song of Mary is both a rallying cry and a promise that a new world order is coming, it could even be considered a defiant protest against what is. Even when Mary's words are beautified in our liturgies and made to sound sweet and ethereal, the power of her God-given voice can never be quenched. However you couch it, saying that the mighty, the rich and the proud are going to be toppled from their seats of power and sent away in shame is never going to be an easy message to proclaim, especially to the rich and powerful, but these are the very words she was given to voice, and the child within her was preparing to embody them.

When the Christ child was born, if this was anything at

all like a normal birth, the first intake of breath kick-started a piercing cry which signified a new human life and shattered the crystal-clear air. With this cry, all creation took note. It's difficult to dissociate the birth of this child from the myths that are perpetuated through the tradition, not least in the Christmas carols that describe this holy infant as tender, mild and obedient, and in the words of Francis Chesterton as a 'child that stirs not in His sleep'.[2] The silent, sleeping baby is all conjecture and possibly just wishful thinking, and perhaps this fully human and fully divine youngling was crying and gasping and gurgling as all babies do. Rather than sleeping peacefully because 'no crying he makes',[3] this little thing was likely making such a noise as to be compared to the voice that broke the cedar trees of Libanus, or the voice of Wisdom, crying out in the street, raising her voice in the squares and at the busiest corners of the city,[4] or this little voice could be compared to a voice speaking through fire, or to a trumpet sounding that 'we shall not all sleep but we shall be changed'.[5] Perhaps the baby Jesus kept the whole village up on the night of his birth and made them all cry. From his newly-minted lips his screaming caused the heavens to quake as the ox and the ass moved away to find a quiet corner. Did Mary, in tiredness and despair, gently sing 'lully, lulla, lullay'[6] as she tried to rock him to sleep? It may well be that the sound of this baby crying was like the sound of the breath of life hovering over the quivering cords of his voice, cords which had been waiting to be plucked like the

[2] 'Here is the Little Door', words Francis Chesterton, music Herbert Howells.
[3] From the second verse of 'Away in a Manger'.
[4] Proverbs 1:20-21.
[5] 1 Corinthians 15:51.
[6] From the 'Coventry Carol', an anonymous sixteenth-century Nativity Carol originating in the Coventry Mystery Play, *The Pageant of the Shearmen and Tailors*.

strings of a harp, eager to sing upon this earth since the very dawn of time.

Apart from only one exception, when the boy Jesus is lost and then found in the temple, we do not hear Jesus' voice represented in the scriptures again until he is about thirty years old. We might wonder what Jesus' voice was actually like. There is nothing written down to describe his voice, the gospels do not record it as either glorious or majestic. We know so many of his words and his stories, his parables, and his conversations, we know what others said about him and to him, but we don't know what he sounded like. We must therefore enter into the sound world of Christ and imagine his voice; the only things we know about Jesus' voice is the geographical and cultural context in which it was heard, what it said and what it had the power to do.

It is generally agreed by historians that Jesus and his disciples primarily spoke Aramaic (Jewish Palestinian Aramaic), the common language of Judea in the first century, most likely with a Galilean dialect distinguishable from that of Jerusalem. But we still learn nothing of his voice or what he sounded like. Was his voice an authoritative voice? Was there something otherworldly about the way he spoke, did he speak loudly or was he softly spoken? Was his voice musical? There must have been some quality in Jesus speaking voice which made people listen and keep awake. He preached and held the attention of thousands who sat around him on the hillside, his voice projecting well through the hot dry air. It is recorded in the Gospel of Luke that Jesus stood up in the temple and unrolled the scroll of the prophet Isaiah and read from it, and people listened to him. He was after all a preacher and teacher. His sermon on the mount and many of his dialogues also suggest he was a natural raconteur, a storyteller, a rhetorician, a public speaker, he was a Rabbi. He made people laugh and cry but none of these things are super-human or super-natural traits, they were legacies of his embodiment and echoes of his culture, they are not qualities of what we might necessarily think of as a 'divine voice', and yet in him, God spoke.

The other thing we know about Jesus from the gospels is that he had not only a speaking voice, but a singing voice. God sings. There are a few occasions when we learn that Jesus sang a hymn, most notably after eating a last supper with his disciples. He would have likely sung psalms, probably Psalms 113-118.[7] We can imagine him and the disciples singing as they walked along the dusty roads in the region around Jerusalem, we can easily imagine him singing the psalms of his faith when he was in the synagogue. On the cross, as he was dying, it is possible to imagine Jesus weakly singing the words of Psalm 22 as they would have been sung in the temple, 'My God, My God, why have you forsaken me?'

A voice from Heaven

There is though, another resonance in the voice of Jesus: the divine register. Jesus speaks with God's voice, like iron in a raging fire.[8] His voice also had the power to heal the sick and raise the dead to life. '*Talitha Cum*', he says to the girl who had fallen asleep: little girl, get up! The words alone are unremarkable, but his voice reached deep into the vortex of death and pulled her back into the land of the living.[9] 'Lazarus, come out' he says in a loud voice, looking up to heaven as his friend walks from the tomb after three days

[7] Psalms 113-118 were traditionally the last part of the Hallel or Praise Psalms.

[8] St Cyril of Alexandria, in his commentary on Luke, in Sermon 142, uses the metaphor of iron being brought into contact with fire to describe the nature of God in Christ. The iron will take on the activity of fire, whilst its nature is still iron.

[9] Mark 5:21-43.

dead.[10] Jesus' voice resounds in the vocative. His speech is always creating new worlds. He rebuked demons, he gave those who had no voice a new voice to sing for joy,[11] and the lame were commanded to take up their bed and walk.[12] His voice turned water into wine,[13] and created enough food to feed five thousand people from five loaves and two fish.[14] With his voice alone he calmed a storm at sea with the words 'Peace, be still', so that even the wind and the waves obeyed him.[15] At the beginning of his ministry all Jesus had to say, like a shepherd calling out to his sheep, was 'follow me' and people dropped everything and followed him, immediately. It was as if they recognised his voice. Of course, in the scriptures we have just the remnant of this voice, the words on the page which were remembered and written down but imagine for a moment you were there, and you could hear his voice with your own ears. Blessed are those who have not heard, and yet have come to believe.

There are two moments in the scriptures when the Voice of the Father reaches down from heaven to speak into the story of the life of Christ. The first is the baptism of Jesus by John in the River Jordan. In a parallel narrative, we should first recall the story of Jesus' cousin, John. To understand John's destiny to be the voice that cries out in the wilderness we turn to Zechariah and Elizabeth, his father and mother. Zechariah had his voice taken away by an angel because he did not believe that he and Elizabeth would ever bear a child together. His cynicism is silenced. When the baby is born he and Elizabeth agree that the child is to take the name John, and at that moment Zechariah receives his voice

[10] John 11:43.
[11] The healing of the deaf man in Mark 8:31-37.
[12] John 5:8.
[13] John 2:1-11.
[14] Mark 6:30-44.
[15] Mark 4:35-40.

back and sings out another prophecy which is used by the church at the beginning of each day in the office of morning prayer: 'Blessed be the Lord God of Israel, for he has looked favourably upon his people and set them free'.[16] Zechariah sings that his son is to prepare the way of the Lord and in the words of the Prophet Isaiah, John is to be the voice of one crying out in the wilderness and he begins sharing the good news around the hill country of Judea. Martin Luther describes John the Baptist as the voice called to proclaim the Voice:

> 'So John declares that he is useful in no other respect than with his voice. And that the whole thing which gives him life and motivates him is to be a voice. Oh that those who follow in John's office would themselves also be so fully engaged in handling the Word of God that they would deserve no other name than that of being a voice, just as John does here!' [17]

Jesus is heralded and announced by John, *'prepare the way of the Lord'* and then at his baptism in the River Jordan, Jesus is affirmed by the voice of God the Father: *'This is my Son, the beloved, with whom I am well pleased'*. Jesus is proclaimed by voices human and divine as the beloved Son of God.

The second significant moment when the Voice of God speaks in the Gospels is in the moment of the Transfiguration, when Jesus ascended the high mountain and spoke with Elijah and Moses. It is once again, a moment of light and sound; Jesus' face was dazzling and bright, glory was all around. A cloud covered them, and a voice came from the cloud, just as it did in days of old, and said *'This*

---

[16] Luke 1:59-80.
[17] Martin Luther's Werke (Weimar, Bohlau, 1883), WA 7:525.

is my Son, the Beloved. Listen to him'. [18] This is the Voice to whom all must listen, they must listen as Jesus tells them of what must soon come to pass, they must listen as he teaches and preaches and as he makes his way to Calvary. The Glory of God resounds in his body and in his voice. When Jesus later says 'My sheep hear my voice' in the Gospel of John, this is a commandment encouraging both recognition and obedience.[19] Within this voice there is a revelation and reconciliation between humanity and God. Within this voice there is glorious and eternal life for those who choose to listen.

The Living Voice

There in the garden, Mary sits weeping at the empty tomb. At first, she does not recognize Jesus; she mistakes him for the gardener. Mary did not properly see the stranger in her midst and her ears were not tuned to his newly resurrected voice. When he speaks to her, she carries on the conversation, her eyes filled with tears because she is still consumed by her grief. She does not hear him. It is only when Jesus calls her by her name, that she recognises her Lord. She hears the Voice. There is suddenly a recognition, which pulls her back to life. In this encounter, Mary is then given a voice, like John the Baptist. As John prepares the way of the Lord, Mary proclaims the way of the Lord. She becomes the first apostle, the first voice to proclaim the words 'He is risen'. She is the herald of the resurrection, and her beautiful feet run to bring the good news to the other disciples with the reality of the risen Christ on her lips. She has heard his voice, which was from the beginning, and that voice changes everything forever. We too are here because we have heard that voice, passed on from generation to generation, and what is that

18   Mark 9:2-13.
19   John 10:27.

voice calling us to do and to be? What is that voice enabling us to speak of or sing of?

In another resurrection appearance, the two disciples on the road to Emmaus also fail to recognize Jesus by his appearance, only recognising him by his actions in the breaking of bread and in his voice as he speaks familiar words. They say to each other 'were our hearts not burning within us as he talked to us on the road and opened the scriptures to us?' [20] The disciples don't record the details of the intellectual enlightenment they experienced, but they do record that the voice of the risen Christ warmed their hearts. After the resurrection, the voice of Christ becomes the means of recognition. His resurrected body speaks with a resurrected voice, it is the same voice, but a different voice, a voice which has journeyed to the depths of hell and risen again, a glorious voice, a majestic voice. To those of us who continue to follow, we know not the physical Jesus, bodily ascended to the Father, but we do know the Christ by this voice, and the way that voice speaks to us and through us and within us, warming our hearts. This unknowing and knowing of the voice of Christ, offers the possibility that this voice can be heard through anyone, anywhere, and at any time. It is a voice which is no longer confined by a body or by a place, it is a voice beyond physicality, beyond time, beyond language. It is a voice which speaks to each one of us just as we are, and just where we are.

Because we don't know what Jesus sounded like we have had to imagine and interpret his voice when it is represented in Liturgy and Music. Within the liturgy, throughout most of the history of the mainstream church, the voice of Christ has only been represented by men. The particularity of Jesus' human gender has shaped how his words have been said and heard within the context of corporate worship, and

[20]   Luke 24:32.

57

this is still so in many parts of the church and within his representations in popular culture.

In the tradition of the music of the church, the voice of Christ, the *Vox Christi*, is very often heard as the deepest and lowest male voice. The richness of the bass voice is the voice chosen to sing the words of Christ in Cantatas and Oratorios and in the Passions of J. S. Bach. Setting his voice in this way brings a kind of comfort, security and solidity. Whilst Christ sings with a bass voice in the expressive recitatives, the Evangelist role is performed by a tenor, a higher male voice in a slightly stricter and more intentional metre. For more modern ears and in more contemporary representations, the voice of Christ in *Jesus Christ Superstar* is styled as a tenor, lyrical and light. These are long held musical conventions, but more contemporary composers have pushed the concept of what the voice of Christ sounds like to test both our sensibilities and our theologies. In his St Luke Passion, James MacMillan directs that the *Vox Christi*, is sung by children, either in unison or in triad. Here is a composer who is deeply respectful to the passion tradition to such an extent that the Passion Chorale '*O Haupt voll Blud und Wunden*' ('O Sacred Head sore wounded') from Bach's St Matthew Passion, is musically referenced in this work. But the tradition of a Bass voice singing the words of Christ is subverted and transcended; 'Christus' is sung by a children's choir and the Evangelist is sung by the chorus. The effect of children singing the words of Christ is unearthly and mystical, it literally makes you sit up in your seat with ears alert as you hear these words in a new way. In an interview about St Luke's Passion, MacMillan says,

'Any Passion that casts Christ as a soloist immediately makes him take human form as an adult male, whereas I wanted to examine his otherness, sanctity and mystery. Employing a children's choir grants a measure of innocence to Christ as the sacrificial lamb, while the vocal line is either in unison or in three parts reflecting the oneness or Trinitarian implications of God.'[21]

Through his music, MacMillan expresses the simple truth that the voice of Christ can transcend gender and might be theologically represented in music as the sound of many voices. Though expressed through the particularity of a human body two thousand years ago, Jesus speaks as the voice of God; the same voice that created the heavens and the earth, the same voice that spoke through a burning bush, the same voice that put a bow in the clouds after the devastation of the flood. When Jesus speaks, he is always speaking with this voice, in the liminal space between heaven and earth, a space beyond any fixed cultural, anthropological or indeed biological norms. This may be why hearing Jesus' words spoken or sung by children or by women or by anyone who is unable to be fixed by tradition or expectation, can be illuminating.

When I read scripture in worship or preside at the eucharist, I am very conscious that sometimes I speak the words Jesus spoke with my own voice, I embody his words. Speaking his words when reading scripture is something we would do well to reflect on. How do we respect these words given to us? How do we tell his parables with our voice? In what kind of 'tone' do we read the words of Christ? Do we read them only in our bodily particularity? We need to read these words with the voice of the heart so that the way in which we speak these words is an expression of our soul and finds itself very close to our vocation to pray. For the priest presiding at the Eucharist, this is a mystery we need to delve

[21] James MacMillan: Interview about St Luke Passion (boosey.com), February 2014.

into, for when we stand at the altar, as well as inhabiting the person of Christ, we also inhabit the *Vox Christi*.

For many years, and according to tradition, the only voice heard speaking the words of Christ in this way was a male voice. So, when the voice speaking Christ's words is not what is expected and not the convention, what effect does that have on the listener and the speaker? The effect of hearing a different voice at the altar can be as illuminating as hearing the *Vox Christi* performed by children in a setting of the Passion. This disjuncture lifts our vision and enables us to see the invisible made visible in new ways. It enables us to imagine that the voice of Christ and indeed the voice of God might be more difficult to define and cage. We can only ever offer an inadequate representation of this voice because the voice of God very often operates beyond the bounds of our senses and our reason.

Voicing liminality

In my beautiful parish church, when I was first grappling with being a priest, I was presented with an Eastward facing altar. This was not my tradition, and not what I was used to. In fact, I don't think I had ever worshipped in a church where the altar was eastward facing, and I couldn't see the face of the priest. The sanctuary of the church was small and compact, it wasn't easy to re-arrange and in this space, to tug and pull and twist the altar and altar rails felt as if it was going against a well-established flow. Drawing on the writing of Peter Brook, the theatre and film director who has an instinctive response to the drama of the liturgy, I decided that the space always wins, and the rite shapes the space. This was the 'stage' I had inherited, and I had to inhabit it rather than try and conform it around me.

In his reflections, Brook speaks of the Holy Theatre as a place where the invisible is made visible, he speaks of the wonder of music coming from 'men in white ties and tails, blowing, waving, thumping and scraping away'.[22] Despite the inadequacy and the absurdness of our physical form, beauty can be created, he says, and 'clumsy men are transformed by an art of possession' which could almost be a way of articulating the twenty sixth of the Thirty-nine Articles of Religion: the unworthiness of the Ministers, hinders not the effect of the sacrament'. [23]

Brook also points out that is it not the conductor who makes the music, but it is the music which is making the conductor and speaking through the conductor. The conductor needs to be open to being transformed, ready to be an instrument for the invisible to speak through their body, so that it may reach those who listen. This description alluding to an actor treading the holy boards of a holy theatre, describes the performer as a player in a place of nobility, purity, seriousness and beauty, for me this is a wonderful way of thinking about how the priest inhabits the holy space of the sanctuary and how their task is to allow the music of Christ, and the voice of Christ speak through them and all their imperfections. The absurdness of our 'ties and tails', the clumsiness of our form, the heaviness of our body and indeed our unworthiness, is enlivened by whose words we speak. If we are open to it, the invisible God takes possession of us and tunes us to speak and sing in that name. Robert Spano, the Conductor of the Atlanta Symphony Orchestra, offers something similar. He says that the pinnacle of conducting is when the orchestra, through your direction, has come to embody the music to such an

[22] 'The Holy Theatre' in *The Empty Space* (1968), Peter Brook (Touchstone, Simon & Schuster, 1968), p. 42.
[23] From the *Book of Common Prayer*, Thirty-nine Articles, XXVI (Cambridge University Press).

extent that you can just be there 'for the ride'. [24] The gift of a conductor is to enable the members of an orchestra or choir to own the music for themselves. In the same article, a musician comments that *A lot of conductors come in and they interpret the piece for you. But the great conductors interpret the piece with you.* The priest at the altar has a similar vocation. The priest at the altar and the preacher in the pulpit have no other vocation than, in the words of John the Baptist via Luther, to be a voice.

Back at my super-cute but intransigent eastward facing altar, who was I to disrupt all of this? I didn't want to change this little gem of a church so I could be 'seen'. I was not the star of this show, I was called to be the conductor who helped everyone else sing, the person who interpreted *with* and not *for*, enabling others to make their own music. I concluded I would have to adapt; I would have to change. So, I became, out of necessity, a priest who had to preside with my back to the people and my face, as it were, to God. At the beginning this felt both rude and aloof from what I was used to, but after a week or two I suddenly realised this way of praying the eucharist afforded me much freedom and thereby I believe it gave the worshipping community freedom too. I was able to perform the liturgy in a different kind of way, largely through my voice, mostly in prayer. On some days it felt like I was leading a charge, on other days it felt like I was leading the way, occasionally it felt like I was running away, but most of the time, thanks be to God, it felt like I had a freedom to pray and face my maker, and because I had this freedom to pray, I was able to gather the prayers of others and place them on the altar as I blessed and broke bread. I was able to let the music transform me. This was my *I-Thou* moment. This was my unconditional turning towards God

[24]   In 'Measure for Measure, exploring the mysteries of conducting', by Justin Davidson in *The New Yorker*, August 2006.

diverted by nothing and I believe this enabled me, in that position, to conduct all other *I-Thou* relations towards God with me.[25]

This manner of presiding imbued a sense of humility and purpose, it somehow gave me focus and let me turn my face to the beautiful reredos depicting the Holy Spirit in the form of a dove coming down out of heaven. It meant that it was indeed my voice which was doing much of the audible work of prayer in public worship. In the Eastward facing celebration of the eucharist, it is the voice which enjoins, and bears and beckons and then carries the prayers of the faithful as an offering to God. Through the intention of my voice and through the grace of the Holy Spirit, I was making the bread and wine the body and blood of Christ, and they were making me.

I am not the only priest to find facing God at the altar, so to speak, liberating. Sarah Coakley explores the position of the priest's body in relation to the eucharist as representing both the people to God and representing God in Christ to the people.[26] The priest, she says, is in some ways always beyond the particularity of their gender in this position and standing in a thin space of liminality and fluidity. I want to take Coakley's conception just a little further and suggest that it is also the voice of the priest being spoken in the sanctuary that shapes and conducts this liminal space through a form of demonstrative and vocal prayer made on behalf of all people. It is not only the position of the body at the altar that creates the music of this sacrifice of praise, but also the voice made from within the body of the priest that makes the invisible visible and orchestrates the prayers of

---

[25] The Post-script added by the author, in *I and Thou*, Martin Buber (T&T Clark, 1958), pp. 133-134.

[26] 'The Woman at the Altar', in *The New Asceticism: Sexuality, Gender and the Quest for God*, Sarah Coakley (Bloomsbury, 2015).

the church between heaven and earth. With all eyes on God, the priest speaks both with the Vox Christi and the Vox Laos, seamlessly moving between one register and another, as a breath between lover and beloved, between bride and bridegroom, between male and female, between the human and divine.

CHAPTER THREE

The Unpredictable Breath of God

The wind blows where it pleases.
You hear its sound,
but you do not know where it comes from or where it goes.
So it is with everyone who is born of the Spirit.
John 3:8

From what we know about God and the way God works, we might conclude that God sometimes chooses to speak in unusual ways, and to and through unusual people. There is quite a lot of evidence for this in the Bible, from the beginning to the end, and in almost every chapter of every book. It is something that is often conveniently forgotten by the church with its traditions and systems and preferences. One might say, it is a besetting sin of the church to put God in a box and perpetuate the myth that God speaks only in established and authorised ways and only through and to established and authorised people. It has never been so. It would, to be frank, be much easier if this were the case, for then we could control God, but this is not how God works and the project of coming to know God is largely about coming to know that God does not do what you expect and very often does not do what you would like.

This is not to say that the orthodoxy of the church is not important, it very much is. We need our creeds and our formulas, we need our doctrines, patterns of prayer and set liturgies, we need our scriptures and sacraments and our right discernments. We need our orders and our authorities. We need our traditions and our ways of living out the faith which are passed on from one generation to another. But, in addition to all these streams of orthodox communication and in addition to all these ways of being and living as the church, God can still choose to work in mysterious ways beyond their bounds.

Much to the chagrin of those who crave order, conformity, power and authority, this means we cannot control God or indeed dictate how or when God speaks, nor to whom God speaks. Augustine was sat in the garden weeping when the voice of a child commanded him to 'take up and read' the words of scripture, leading to his conversion to Christianity. Mary Ward, the Catholic nun and social reformer, was combing her hair when a voice spoke to her of the glory of God, 'Glory, glory, glory' it said, inspiring her ministry enabling girls and women to access education. Very often, the 'proper channels' become the towers and temples which must be reduced to dust so that God can be set free from our human conventions and expectations. God is like the wind, like fire, like a bird, uncatchable, uncontainable. Michael Ramsey in his reflections on the Holy Spirit, comments that the church's continuity through history is shaped by the sacraments, the apostolic ministry and the teaching of the church, and the Holy Spirit uses this shape to reveal the works of God. But, he warns, the Holy Spirit also acts in unpredictable ways, 'exposing, teaching, illuminating, judging, renewing'. The Sprit he says, is still as it was and ever shall be, the unpredictable breath of God.[1] The bottom line is, God will never conform, and God can be extremely unorthodox and untraditional. From the

[1] Michael Ramsey, *Holy Spirit* (SPCK, 1977), 'Spirit, Fellowship, Church', Chapter 6, p. 86.

beginning God took a swerve away from established routes and ostentatious religiousness and has instead chosen, again and again, to speak directly to the unusual, the outsider, the small and the insignificant and has spoken to them, and through them, freely and lovingly.

The Noisy Prayers of Loud Women

Every year Hannah and her husband Elkanah, the Ephraimite, along with his other wife Penninah, went to the temple at Shiloh.[2] Hannah was unable to conceive; her womb was closed, and in her barrenness, she was taunted by Penninah and was desolate and bitter in soul. She would have been an outcast, the woman who could not bear children, she would have been positioned on the edge of respectability and community, and in her desperation, she goes alone to stand before the Lord in the temple. The priest, Eli, kept to his station at the doorposts, watching from a distance, looking down upon Hannah with the condescending gaze of officialdom. All Eli could see was a 'hysterical' woman in much turmoil, her lips were moving, her head was bowed, tears were running from her eyes, but we are told her voice could not be heard, she was praying in her heart to the Lord. Naturally, Eli thought she was drunk, and he tells her to sober up. It is as if Eli has not seen anyone fervently praying before despite his years of temple service. Perhaps he was fearful of the woman, perhaps he was just straightforwardly condemnatory, maybe he had only ever seen people praying the established and accepted prayers of the temple and not their own. Was this the first thought of a holy man towards any woman, or towards anyone who hovered outside or just beyond the temple sacrifices and temple walls? Hannah finds her voice and she tells Eli the cause of her dejection and the hope of her prayers. Her prayers are later answered

[2]   The First book of Samuel, Chapter 1.

in the birth of a son, Samuel, whom she offers to the Lord in gratitude for having heard her crying. When Samuel is a little older, we find him in the temple serving the Lord in the presence of Eli, but we learn that at that time it was rare for the Lord to speak; visions were uncommon. Samuel had no personal experience of the Lord and so he is rather confused when he hears a voice from beyond speaking to him, but eventually he can respond: 'Speak Lord, for your servant is listening'. God subverts the usual channels of expected communication, and rather than speaking to and through the old priest, Eli, God speaks to and through the young boy Samuel.

In the Gospels we often see Jesus acting in similarly unpredictable ways, speaking to those outside the chosen and well-established religious community; the prostitutes, the tax-collectors, the sick and the lame. The woman at the well is a good and pointed example.[3] Here is a woman who comes to collect water in the heat of the day and meets Jesus at Jacob's well. Here is a woman who is a Samaritan, she is probably a social outcast and has had five men, *and the one you now have is not your husband,* Jesus observes. She does not know who Jesus is, but she is inquisitive about his identity and asks a series of straightforward questions. Despite her apparent ignorance she senses something 'other' and shows respect. The Samaritan woman says what she thinks and as they talk to one another, she comes to believe that Jesus is Messiah. She goes back to her village and tells of this man who knew everything about her: the good and the bad, in fact, he told her everything she had ever done. You can imagine her, the outcast, suddenly at the centre of the community telling her story with gusto, her testimony bringing many others to believe. In the Orthodox tradition, the woman at the well is given a name, *Photini,* meaning 'enlightened one', and she

[3] John 5:5-26.

is one of the first people in the Gospel of John to proclaim the good news and bear witness to Christ, an equal to the apostles. That name, the enlightened one, suggests she is someone who sees things as they are and indeed says things as they are without any dissemblance. Her story also reminds us that Christ speaks to whomsoever he wishes to speak, and he acts in unpredictable ways; exposing, teaching, illuminating, judging, renewing.

At the edges of establishment

In the crypt of York Minster there lies the last shrine of William Fitzherbert, otherwise known as St William of York. His history and rather unremarkable hagiography, as we have received it, is of a rich man of noble birth, buffeted by the partisan politics of his day, a good man who felt called to serve as Archbishop of York, as chief pastor to his flock (though he was the third choice, and his election was alleged to have been corrupt). His appointment was thwarted by mobs of Cistercian monks with whom he had a long running antipathy, and they to him; he was deposed, exiled, and then reappointed. On his way back to York, the bridge over the River Ouse collapsed as he and his entourage entered the city, thankfully and miraculously no one was hurt. Upon his return, William was probably murdered by the Archdeacon of York who poisoned the chalice as he celebrated mass on 8 June, in the year 1154.

Far from a perfected picture of sainthood, William's life was more complex, more ordinary and even for a man of those times, pretty underwhelming. History suggests he was neither a particularly talented clergyman nor a wholly inspirational figure during his lifetime, but neither of those things prevented him from archiepiscopacy (twice). His reputation was both wonderful as a good and faithful pastor, but also tarnished. His story is chequered with intrigue and crowned with a number of reported miracles during his life and a couple of others which flowered from his sweet-smelling shrine at York Minster, leading to his canonisation in the year 1226.[4] One can't help wondering if this reflected the economic need for a saint associated with the Cathedral, and so became a cause and justification for veneration and pilgrimage. However, venerated as William was, his cult never expanded significantly beyond York, but his shrine did become a popular spiritual destination for those seeking miracles or prayers.

Nevertheless, the concern here is not William of York directly, but one of those tourists-cum-pilgrims who came to visit his shrine and pray 'quietly' in the Minster in 1413, and again in 1417, someone who was beyond the fringe of the church and had to find her own ways and means of praying. At that time, the Shrine of St William of York would have been well worth a visit by any serious spiritual pilgrim and Margery Kempe was a serious pilgrim (almost a professional) and a serious seeker. She may also have travelled to see the newly completed Great East Window, depicting scenes from the book of Genesis and the Book of Revelation, which was completed in 1408. She may have come to see the window dedicated to St William installed in 1415. There was plenty to see and do to make a trip to York worthwhile.

In juxtaposition to the establishment figure of William Fitzherbert and the church he inhabited, here is an ordinary woman of deep and exceptional faith, who was rarely taken seriously by the clerical classes of the day. Despite their attempts to silence her she continued unperturbed in her personal spiritual quest for holiness. She was drawn to the church but was always on the periphery, like someone constantly knocking at the door wanting to be let in. Here was

---

[4] *St William of York*, Christopher Norton (York Medieval Press, University of York, 2006), pp. 1, 2.

someone who didn't speak in fine or poetic language, instead she spoke in the rough, coarse language of the people. Here was someone who was as flighty and as spontaneous and as unpredictable as the wind, blowing where it willed. Here was someone who, in complete faith and trust in God, felt that she had every right and justification to pray and worship in the grandest cathedrals and abbeys, and was permitted to speak the words of Christ as much as anyone else in Christendom. Her pulpit was the rough and tumble of daily living, it was the streets of the cities she visited; her followers seemed to be made up of all the other people knocking at the door trying to get into the inner sanctuary of the church. She feared no one, she judged no one. In an ecclesiastical world of power, intrigue and obfuscation, Margery Kempe was simply herself. She always came before the living God just as she was, in naked honesty without pomp or pretence. Against convention, she committed herself and her husband to a chaste marriage after bearing many children, which served to free her for unaccompanied spiritual adventures whilst he remained at home in Norfolk, presumably changing nappies.

Just before her first trip to York, Christ spoke to her and said that those who heard her, were hearing the voice of God.[5] In her own dictated accounts of her experiences (for Kempe could not read or write very much), she vividly describes not only her journeys to churches, holy houses, spiritual sites and shrines all over the world, but also her conversations with Christ, with whom she would speak as both Lord and friend, confidant, conscience and Almighty Creator. Kempe was not the quiet, prayerful, obedient virgin the church would have liked her to be. Neither was she an obedient wife. She was a mother of fourteen, a businesswoman, a brewer, and more troubling than any of those things, she had a mind of her own

[5]   Margery Kempe, *The Book of Margery Kempe*, translated by Barry Windeatt (Penguin, 1985; 2019), Chapter 10, p. 27.

and said not only what she thought, but also what she believed Christ to be saying to her. She was always the enlightened outsider who was paradoxically always at the centre of the community. She was an earthy creature, and she was noisy in her prayers which were often made manifest through loud wailing and tears, for noisy weeping was her charism. If it were not for the fact that she didn't drink alcohol at all, there would have been every chance she might have been perceived as being drunk by those who guarded the doors of the temple. She was someone for whom the word 'loquacious' would have been an understatement and for the church, in all its self-righteous up-tightness, these characteristics were both a threat and a curiosity, with clerics being variously appalled and enchanted by her.

Upon her second visit to York, Margery took communion in the Minster on the Sunday morning, and she records that she, always referring to herself in the third person as 'God's creature', received communion with 'much weeping, violent sobbing and loud crying, so that many people wondered very much what was wrong with her'.[6] After this episode she was ordered to appear before some of the cathedral canons (some of my ancient predecessors), and local doctors of divinity. She was marched into the Chapter House, an intimidating space even today, and being encircled by her accusers, her faith and understanding of it were tested. She was then sent for a 'chat' with the Archbishop of York who would finally be able to arbitrate upon any alleged heresies of which she had been suspected. The thing that seemed to bother the Archbishop most was that people listened to Margery's voice. It was as if she had a natural authority all of her own. There was truth in what she said and often a cutting clarity. The crowds listened to her testimony and who knows how many people she brought to

6   Ibid.

belief. She knew the gospels and spoke of Christ intimately, so she was then accused of preaching, a heinous crime for one such as her, and she was reminded that according to St Paul no woman should preach, no woman should speak, and no woman should have a voice. Margery opined that all she was doing was speaking of God. All she was doing was just as the Samaritan woman at the well did, she was speaking of her own experience of Christ and sharing what he said to her with anyone who would listen. Wasn't that what Christ asked of everyone?

In the end, at every questioning, Kempe's honesty and authenticity was undefeated though she was sent away by a seemingly flummoxed Archbishop, and cautioned never to return to the Diocese of York.[7] This small episode in the extraordinary life of Margery Kempe is a vignette that exposes the layers of power running over centuries through the life of the church. Women like Margery represented all those who fell outside of the usual power structures who nevertheless walked the way of holiness and prayed to God in their own way. A few decades on, a Margery would have probably been tried as a witch, condemned for speaking out, having a mind of her own and questioning the authority and wisdom of the men around her. It's a miracle really that she navigated her relatively long life from 1373-1438 without any tragic mishaps as she criss-crossed the globe speaking freely, on a life-long pilgrimage of faith.

A vision of the church through personal encounter

Margery was a very different character to her fellow Norfolk-woman, Julian of Norwich (1343-1416). Margery found her

---

[7] Ibid, Chapter 50, 51 and 52, p. 121.

freedom and independence in faith (one could say she found her voice), through travel and pilgrimage. She presents herself as a prize-winning extrovert. Julian, on the other hand, found her voice by incarcerating herself and living the life of an anchoress. Julian received many visitors and pilgrims who sought her out for spiritual counsel, including Margery who is said to have visited her in Norwich in 1413. Mother Julian was also someone to whom God spoke beyond the bounds of the established church, and she was also someone who spoke of God and what God in Christ was saying to her personally through a series of revelations or 'showings'. We know much less about Mother Julian's character, but her visions are vivid, emotive, and often challenging. Her work was neglected for centuries, and when her book was first published in 1670, it was not warmly received by the Anglican establishment with her writing being described among 'the fantastic revelations of distempered brains'.[8] Julian and Margery were women who were always at the edges of the established church and yet each in their own way expanded the vision of what the Body of Christ could be. Margery's ecclesiology, if you will, challenges the church to be more authentic to those whom it is called to serve, even resembling the proposed mission statement of the Church of England today, in which the church calls itself to be 'simpler, humbler and bolder'. Julian's ecclesiology is much more complex, but it has been proposed as a theology of the body politic experienced through an isolated body and offers a vision of the church which is called to suffer with Christ whilst at the same time being fully redeemed by his love.

[8]   A quote from the Anglican Bishop, Edward Stillingfleet, in his work *A Discourse concerning the idolatry practiced in the church of Rome and the hazard of Salvation in the Communion of it: In answer to some Papers of a Revolted Protestant. Wherein a Particular account is given of the fanaticisms and divisions of the church*, 2nd ed. (London, 1672), p. 224 in *Julian of Norwich and the mystical body politic of Christ*, Frederick Christian Bauerschmidt (University of Notre Dame Press, 1999) p. 1.

The Book of Margery Kempe, though dictated, is noted as the first autobiography ever written in English, but Julian of Norwich is credited with writing one of the earliest known works in the English language by the hand of a woman. The stories of Margery Kempe and Julian of Norwich amongst very likely, many other medieval mystics and outcasts, cause us to consider the God who speaks directly to the hearts and souls of those beyond the established and expected confines of the church.

Their writings also cause us to reflect on where the central locus of the church was in their time and in ours. For now, as then, the church still looks with suspicion and caution upon those who profess their own reality of a God who is able to speak directly to them. As I reflect on the lives of Margery and Julian, I can't help wondering whether these two women would be taken any more seriously in the twenty-first century, than they were in the fifteenth. How are voices like theirs heard and incorporated into the orthodoxy of the church today? Who has the authority to judge whether the voice of God in any person's life is orthodox or heretical? Who are the figurative 'women at the well' in today's world and does the church ever listen to them? Who are the boys like Samuel, who do not know the Lord at all, but hear the Lord's voice calling to them? Ultimately, the question we are encouraged to ask through their witness is, where is the church and who is the church for? How is the *Body of Christ* made real, in the places of our world where the religious language and systems we are so used to, have broken down or become unknown?

I am always conscious that I am part of the tradition of the established church. The traditions of the church are important to me, but I suppose we all need to be alert to our traditions becoming 'fossilized' as Michael Ramsey might have put it. It's not unusual to see God in Christ at work beyond the church and beyond the established forms and orthodoxies we promote. Sometimes these occasions of revelation happen in the ordinary places of life, at the hairdressers, the school, the supermarket, the pub, and the places where we gather water daily. Sometimes these revelations happen during extraordinary moments in history when everything changes and everything has to change, when the direction of the world seems to shift, and things have to be realigned. At these moments the church might sometimes set itself free from its inherited religious structures and systems for a moment and simply respond as the Body of Christ in the world. You get a sense of two different manifestations of the church in the lived theology of Margery Kempe and Julian of Norwich, both of whom, in their own very particular way, embodied a new vision for the church revealed to them by the voice of Christ as the established church looked on nervously.

Where is God?

During the global pandemic of 2020, the usual structures and established patterns of prayer and orthodoxy were broken down, we couldn't even go into a church to pray as priest or people. Despite the best efforts of privileged congregations to go 'on-line', essentially the Christians of the world were on their own, at home with their own thoughts and their own prayers, their own voices and visions, their own ways of praying and living as the Body of Christ in isolation. The Body of Christ was atomised. We had to create our own patterns of prayer. This left many of us wondering, when we are distanced from the formal prayers of the church, or indeed excluded from them, for whatever reason, how do we pray? When we are beyond the structures of the establishment, with its set liturgies and statutory prayers and places which are set aside, how do we pray? When we are excluded from the church because of who we are or what we believe, or when we feel we cannot enter a church for fear of judgement or abuse, how do we pray? When the language of prayer is exclusive and divisive, how do we pray? When the church is fragmented and dispersed whether through plague or famine or war or schism, how do we Christians pray as one?

At the beginning of his career, the German theologian, Dietrich Bonhoeffer remarked that 'The concept of the Church is conceivable only in the sphere of reality established by God; this means it cannot be deduced.'[9] He suggests that we can never predict or dictate where the church might come to exist or where, or in whom, Christ may choose to abide. Somewhat ironically, Bonhoeffer spent his whole life directed to the very task of deducing and discerning the concept of the church in relation to the reality of the world established by God. This ultimately forced Bonhoeffer to accept that neither he, nor humankind can direct where the church will be found and cannot bind the earthly manifestation of God's Church in the world with the shackles and restrictions of religion.

In his *Letters and Papers from Prison*, Bonhoeffer seems to catch a glimpse of a church which is greater than any human form of religion and suddenly sees a vision of a universal church that stands not where human powers and humanity give out, but rather a church which exists at 'the very centre of the village' and in the 'midst of our life' as human beings in the world.

It could be said that the turmoil which Bonhoeffer witnessed in the world and experienced through his own personal sufferings, serves not only to intensify but also to clarify and strengthen his theological commitments.

---

[9]   Dietrich Bonhoeffer, *Sanctorum Communio: A Theological Study of the Sociology of the Church* (1517 Media; Fortress Press; 1998), p. 127.

Bonhoeffer never gives up on the idea of the Church as Christ existing as community. What is perhaps shocking to him, his readers and to us today, is that he finds that Christ existing as community is not always in the most obvious place. In extremis, the empirical church, if it is unable to suffer with the world and serve the world, is not necessarily the place where God chooses to reveal Godself. The Body of Christ is to be found elsewhere, where there is suffering, where there is despair, where there is doubt and confusion and where there is mess and unpredictability. Is the church to be found in the shrine itself, in the lives of the people who gather around it, or indeed in the lives of the people stood at the door, waiting to be let in?

In a way, dear Margery Kempe in all of her loud crying and raucousness and in all of the ways in which she subverted the establishment, and blesséd Julian of Norwich in her self-isolation and silence, both remind us that the Body of Christ is to be found, and the voice of Christ is to be heard, in the most unlikely places and people, each one a different kind of shrine or temple to God in our midst. In their singular pursuit of faith and through their personal relationship with God, they point the whole church towards a vocation of truth-telling and love-making. Margery is guileless to obfuscation, dissembling and cloaking; an innocent abroad who lets God speak through her. Julian, through her suffering sees only love as the meaning of the universe and as the foundation of faith in Christ. As well as nurturing tradition and clinging on to establishment, the Church of today will become more confident in its own voice if it is able to hear the unpredictable voices of those enlivened, as Michael Ramsey says, by the unpredictable breath of God.

CHAPTER FOUR

How Can I Keep From Singing?

It is the voice of the Church that is heard in
singing together.
It is not you that sings, it is the Church that is singing,
and you, as a member of the Church, may share in its song.
Dietrich Bonhoeffer, Life Together

The first time I went to a football match I was convinced that tens of thousands of people singing in unison was enough to turn the game. I had never heard such visceral and uninhibited singing, or such power mediated by song. The combined will and energy of a myriad of voices, it seemed to me, could really be enough to encourage and inspire tired bodies at the end of the second half to give it one final push in extra time and come away as victors. I would go as far as to say that the experience of being in the midst of a wall of sound and in the middle of thousands of voices conjoined in song, was almost a spiritual one. Not all the words of the songs were *spiritually edifying*, by any means, but the energy of this sound was glorious. Some of the football chants were sung to tunes that I vaguely knew. Fragments of them emerged in waves during the course of the game: 'Eventide' ('Abide with me'), 'When the Saints go marching in', and 'Cwm Rhonnda'. I was swept up in the romance of massed voices, the novelty of which distracted me from the actual words being sung, which were often neither virtuous nor kind.

The singing I experienced that day was spontaneous, unrehearsed and in all honesty not that advanced, but the 1927 Cup Final between Cardiff City and Arsenal was preceded by a designated session of community singing, the activity arising from the Community Singing Movement of the 1920s. 'Abide with me' was the royally ordained hymn to be sung by all supporters and was to be the climax of the pre-match singing session, presenting a rather wholesome picture of *'the nation as family made flesh'*.[1] The Community Singing Movement was an attempt to instil a sense of feel-good, moral improvement in the general population and saw singing as a means of building community spirit, albeit in a particular political direction; the sponsor of the movement was none other than the *Daily Express*.[2] Though some saw the movement as simply a gimmick and a means to increase circulation of the newspaper, a correspondent at the said Cup Final waxed lyrical about the singing football crowd much as I have at the beginning of this chapter; he said the experience was uplifting and spiritual. 'I realised' he said, 'that deep in the souls of all of us, is a love of song and singing.'[3]

Supporters of the movement claimed that singing bound people together, and at a time of growing disparity between the classes and a growing gap between rich and poor, community music and song were seen as balm to social ills or (more cynically), as a gloss to cover over growing inequalities. Not long after the thrill of the Cup Final in 1927 (Cardiff City-1 Arsenal-0), the movement began to wane and eventually the thought of tens of thousands of

[1] Russell, Dave, 'Abiding Memories: The Community Singing Movement and English Social Life in the 1920s.' Popular Music, vol. 27, no. 1 (Cambridge University Press, 2008), pp. 117–33, http://www.jstor.org/stable/40212447
[2] Ibid.
[3] *Daily Express*, 25 April 1927.

fans being coerced into singing merrily together before a football match became a futile exercise in attempting to enforce jollity. Imagine the embarrassment rippling around a stadium in an invisible wave of resistance and murmuring. Modern day football crowds don't try to be anything that they're not. Football chants are not meant to be edifying, they are expressions of support for your team or indeed for the disparagement of the opposition, and are far from an exercise in moral improvement.

Uplifting musical experiences can of course still be had at major sporting fixtures when a national anthem is sung or another song which evokes nostalgia and pride among those who are singing; songs such as 'Land of Hope and Glory', 'Rule, Britannia!' and 'Jerusalem' would easily fall into this category. I remember getting a free ticket to an evening of athletics at the Commonwealth Games held in Manchester in 2002, and in that context we sang 'Land of Hope and Glory' as a substitute national anthem for the England team (it was replaced by Jerusalem in 2010). It was certainly rousing, but I felt uneasy singing of a God who made a nation 'mighty' and who would make us 'mightier yet'. I felt that ship had long sailed and for someone like me, at the beginning of new millennium, the concept and language of empire was one I found uncomfortable.[4] So I mumbled those words because I didn't feel I could sing them wholeheartedly. Because singing is such a physical and emotive experience and an activity which seems to require the whole of your being: body, mind, and spirit, how can you sing something that you don't quite believe or know to be true? I find that singing something that I don't quite

[4]   A full exploration of the connections between corporate song and the relationship between music and empire and the cultural life of the United Kingdom is explored in *Music and Empire: Britain 1876-1953*, Jeffrey Richards (Manchester University Press, 2001).

believe in to be both a cognitive and embodied dissonance, I somehow feel discordant within myself. There are hymns I have been presented with over the years that I find difficult to sing because the words have been dated, careless, exclusive, or presented a particular theological perspective I could not align myself with. What we sing, and why we sing it, really does matter. Chine McDonald in *God is Not a White Man*, reflects on the 1984 Band Aid charity single 'Do They Know it's Christmas?', and the damage that can be perpetuated by uncritical mass song.[5] McDonald questions the position from which the song came, that of colonial white 'missions' and patronal benevolence. Africans quite obviously *knew* it was Christmas, she says, because Christianity in Africa was more vibrant and integral to the life of that continent than Christianity in the United Kingdom. In the end, this was a song that McDonald had to stop singing. We are reminded again and again that the words and intentions of a song matter over and above whether it has a catchy tune.

From the sports stadia we could journey on to the concert hall and specifically the great British tradition of the *Last Night of the Proms*, when the vestiges of empire and nationalism are sung with pomp and circumstance and the waving of flags. This annual music festival regularly gets caught up in the so called 'culture wars', when questions are raised about what kind of music we should be singing together on such occasions and what kind of intentions or associations such blatantly nationalistic music stirs up within us. If corporate singing indicates what team someone belongs to, and thereby expresses an identity, what kind of identity is being expressed becomes important. In a post-colonial world where persistent and violent remnants of our imperial past are still being used to quash the voices of those who bore the

---

[5] Chine McDonald, *God Is Not a White Man, and Other Revelations* Hodder and Stoughton, 2021), p. 76.

pain of this history most, might we need to be careful what we sing and dare we reframe and re-orchestrate these songs for a new kind of nation? Songs which had once been an expression of solidarity had become an expression of division and the pawn of those who sought to divide the nation further for their own political ends.[6] Just a few years later, the Proms were again a focus for criticism, as it was noted that the majority of the flags being waved on the last night were those of the European Union, suggesting that some of the singing about how 'mighty' this small island nation was, may have been verging on the ironic as the musicians on stage, from all over Europe, and indeed from all over the world, shared their music in the Royal Albert Hall.

From the concert hall we could move on to national events and celebrations whereupon the population is called to sing in unison to give thanks or to express sorrow: jubilees, armistice days, coronations, anniversaries, royal weddings and funerals. The National Anthem, with its anonymously written music and words and relatively modern origin, still effectively gathers the nation together in song but when we sing 'God Save the King', those four words alone make several assumptions about our beliefs, our politics, and our conception of what it means to be British. The first time I sang those particular words, soon after the death of Queen Elizabeth II, I found it hard not to be intensely moved by what is essentially a prayer of invocation and petition. The sudden change of one word, carried the shaken identity of a nation and its raw grief.

From here we could move on to the corporate song that we still just about manage to express in school assemblies or at the funerals, weddings, and civic occasions within our own communities, when the church can become one of a

[6]   Culture wars in the UK: division and connection, (May 2021) Policy Institute, King's College London and Ipsos MORI.

few designated spaces in our society for community singing, but it must be said, with an ever-decreasing repertoire and engagement. Christmas is perhaps the one time during the year when the community reclaims its voice and the carols once sung in pubs and on the streets by wassailers are gentrified in services of Nine Lessons and Carols and sung by increasing numbers of people as a way of marking their festive celebrations. The most popular services in churches and cathedrals are carol services and if people can sing 'Hark the Herald' and 'O Come, All Ye Faithful', they go home happy, having perhaps done with church and done with singing, until the next year.

We could move further to the week by week gathering of the faithful remnant for whom singing is a cornerstone of their offering of worship, just so long as the vicar has chosen a good tune that everyone knows. Even the timeless image of bulging congregations singing hymns lustily as they do on *Songs of Praise*, is fading fast. Many churches can barely rally a choir, or a worship group, or an organist and either don't sing at all or sing along to CDs or Spotify playlists specially designed for karaoke congregations and pumped through weak speakers. At the other end of the spectrum, for those who can afford it, professional musicians sing on behalf of the people, who stand in silence as the 'Gloria', the church's hymn of praise, is sung for them, sometimes in Latin. Or alternatively, just to reflect the current breadth of the singing church, a different kind of professional musician stands at the front of the church with a guitar, leading an assembly not unlike a scene from the Pyramid stage at Glastonbury.

As I stood in the temple of Old Trafford that day, I had one wish: that one day the singing in our churches could be as uninhibited, as passionate and as whole-hearted. I longed for congregations to be as fervent in their song as these football fans were in theirs. I longed for our churches to sing with the Spirit and with the understanding also. I began to wonder whether the church in the west had forgotten how to sing, and whether the joy of corporate song was somehow ebbing away, not only from our wider communities but also from many of the acts of worship through which our faith was expressed. Our song was becoming disembodied, fragmented, and atomised; we were losing our confidence to sing, and we were losing our voice.

Some years later, as I led funeral services at the local crematorium, or weddings in church, I was often the only voice singing. I felt like one of the conductors of the erstwhile Community Singing Movement whose chief task was to enthuse the reluctant crowd to sing. I was basically acting as an animateur. Most of the time it seemed part of my vocation was to offer vicarious song on behalf of everyone else who looked down at their feet, or mumbled into their hymn book, or who just seemed utterly embarrassed by this singing thing. Over the years it has become increasingly difficult to encourage hymn singing at all at funerals, and grieving congregations seem more comfortable remaining silent as Frank Sinatra sings 'My Way' for them, or Andrea Bocelli sings 'Time to say Goodbye'. At one memorable wedding, the couple had asked if the final hymn could be 'O Happy Day'. Now this is a wonderfully inspiring hymn written by Phillip Doddridge in 1755, but I think the bride and groom had in their minds eye the Gospel arrangement by the Edwin Hawkins Singers (1969) or a cover of the same by Aretha Franklin (1987) or most likely a scene from *Sister Act 2*. To be fair, they had a vision like I did. When they came to the altar to declare their love for each other and have it blessed by God, they too had a dream of the whole church singing and the congregation erupting in unbridled joy. I got that. I felt bad trying to dissuade them from this course of action, for as their priest I had come

85

to understand that the church was fast losing its voice and the cultural practice of singing was waning, but my gentle protestations were to no effect. After the great celebration of their marriage, the organ struck up, the robed choir began to sing rather uncomfortably, and the congregation of this average Manchester suburb were bemused and shuffled in their shiny suits and posh dresses. There was no clapping or swaying and certainly no syncopation, there was just a pool of benevolent awkwardness. Thankfully, after that disappointment they walked out of the church to Mendelsohn's 'Wedding March' which did the trick, so everything was all right in the end. But the gap between our hope of how the church might sing and offer praise and how it does sing (perhaps metaphorically as well as literally) is getting wider and wider. If singing is an expression or sign of belief, if it is a sign and symbol of the church itself, which I want to say it is, Christianity in this country, both the knowledge of it and adherence to it, is no longer something that the general population are willing or often able, to sing in support of.

What song can do

The power of corporate song offered with a common purpose and shared belief is well exemplified in what came to be known as the Singing Revolution of Estonia towards the end of the Cold War.[7] Along with Latvia and Lithuania who were also suppressed and annexed by Russia, the nation of Estonia (long known for its love of song), rose up in defiance. The history of song in Estonia reaches far into its national history, runic folk songs were passed down aurally from generation to generation and by the thirteenth century the

[7]   The term 'Singing Revolution' was coined by the Estonian activist and artist Heinz Valk in 1988 who said, 'A nation who makes its revolution by singing and smiling, should be a sublime example to all.'

tradition of liturgical song and hymn singing via the Roman and then Lutheran churches had also been embedded in the culture. Singing was a normal daily activity for children and families and particularly for men, it happened in schools, in homes and in the workplace, the same is so for the thriving Christian communities across the church in Africa today, singing is culturally accepted and encouraged and would often just erupt from nowhere and in beautiful harmonies. This music of the people was intrinsically linked to personal and national identities to such an extent that these songs, containing stories, language and culture became vessels of liberation. The tradition of choral singing was embedded in Estonian society, and singing together was, and still is, an important part of its own cultural heritage and understanding.[8] Everyone was expected to be part of a choir and choral singing was celebrated at ever-popular choral festivals throughout the nineteenth and twentieth centuries, which survived world wars and ongoing occupation. In 1988, over 300,000 Estonians (more than one third of the total population of the country) gathered in Tallinn to sing together in peaceful protest against their Russian occupiers. This moment in history was regarded as a turning point in the country's journey towards self-determination and became known as the Singing Revolution; a form of non-violent resistance where the song was mightier than the sword.

There have been other singing revolutions where music has inspired, encouraged, and consoled those fighting for their freedoms. To sing together is an act of solidarity, making many voices heard where one voice would be ignored. Martin Luther King described song as the 'soul' of

---

[8] 'Joint singing as a means of cultural transmission in Estonia',
Inge Raudsepp, Anu Sepp, Inkeri Roukonen in *Society, Integration, Education Volume II, 452* (ru.lv).

the civil rights movement.[9] The songs were embedded in the history of those who had been enslaved but gave hope to the determination that 'We shall overcome, Black and White together, we shall overcome someday'. King also recognised that God had blessed human beings with a creative capacity and from this capacity has flowed sweet songs of sorrow and joy that enabled human beings to face the challenges that beset them. This observation could easily apply to the Psalter, the hymn book of the Hebrew people. These are the sweet songs of sorrow and joy that the church is called to sing every day. Journeying through all one hundred and fifty psalms over a month reveals a canon of song which expresses every human emotion and all ranges of human condition whether singular or corporate. Dietrich Bonhoeffer said in his reflections on the Psalms, that 'Whenever the Psalter is abandoned, an incomparable treasure is lost to the Christian Church. With its recovery will come unexpected power'.[10] The emotions of the lost and the lonely, the oppressed and the raging, the jubilant and the joyful, the despairing, the displaced and the dying are all represented in the Psalter. They can be sung by a lone voice or by thousands to express sorrow, solidarity or liberation as well as giving voice to the condition of praise to which we are all called. The dynamics of the psalter range from the vibrancy of a congregation in

---

[9]   The evolution of music in the Black freedom struggle reflects the evolution of the movement itself. Calling songs 'the soul of the movement,' King explained in his 1964 book *Why We Can't Wait* that civil rights activists 'sing the freedom songs today for the same reason the slaves sang them, because we too are in bondage and the songs add hope to our determination that "We shall overcome, Black and white together, We shall overcome someday"'. (King, Why, 86).

[10]   Dietrich Bonhoeffer, *The Psalms: 'The Prayerbook of the Bible'* pp. 117, 162 (Augsburg Fortress Press, 1996), as part of *Dietrich Bonhoeffer Works*.

Psalm 150 'let everything that has breath praise the Lord', to the whisper and despair of a lone voice in Psalm 22, with some of the last words that Jesus sang from the cross, 'My God, my God why have you forsaken me'. [11]

Throughout salvation history, singing and song have been at the heart of the human relationship with God enabling a dialogue between the creator and creation. Song is the vehicle for praise: Moses and Miriam sing their song to God in the Book of Exodus; in Luke's Gospel Mary sings her 'Yes' to God in the words of the Magnificat; the Angels sing the Good News of Christ's birth; Anna and Simeon burst into song when they see the Christ Child and the hosts of heaven sing the praises of the Lamb in the Book of Revelation. But it is perhaps in the Book of Psalms, where the singing community is most evident and there is regularly a call to come before the Lord's presence with a song.[12]

The word 'psalm' is derived from the Greek *Psalmoi*, which means 'to be sung with a harp' as part of Hebrew worship. Some psalms were written as community laments, songs for festivals and celebrations, or songs of pilgrimage. The psalms were used to express the hopes, desires, failures, and fears of a whole community of faith and consolidate and imprint its identity. The place of singing within the liturgy was important for the psalmist and often there are specific instructions to indicate how and by whom, the psalms should be performed.[13] The psalms represented the embodiment of praise and the expression of the soul, a precursor to the hymns and spiritual songs that would later evolve in the life

[11] Matthew 27:46.
[12] Psalm 95, 98 and 100 are just three examples.
[13] For example Psalm 50 and 73-83 are preceded by the words 'for the director of music'. Psalm 55 begins *'For the director of music, with stringed instruments.'*

of the early church. Thomas Merton says that it is in the psalms that we 'drink divine praise at its pure and stainless source, in all its primitive sincerity and perfection'.[14] Within the early church, psalms, hymns and spiritual songs were to be sung together. The psalms were the voice of the church. The congregation was the choir. For the first two hundred years or so, it is likely that everyone sang, men, women, children, believers and non-believers on the fringes of faith. The theological ideal of the church was to sing together, and be gathered up like the grains of wheat from the hillside and made into one bread, one singing body.

What we are left with in all these examples is an understanding of the primacy of the text within the context of song. We don't know that much about the tunes of the psalms or of the songs and spiritual songs of the early church, but from the words we have been left and from the words on the pages of our sacred scriptures we can recognise that the intention to praise and offer petition through song was a vital part of the church's life. This wasn't just singing for singing's sake. This was singing with a single-minded intention. Singing for the purpose of praise. A song where the words are at odds with the intention of the heart just won't do and can't be easily sung, for it would be like betraying the self. St Augustine understood the effect of words and music but noted where the real power was. He said, 'I realise it is not the singing that moves me but the meaning of the words when they are sung in a clear voice to the most appropriate tune.' [15]

To sing these songs of the heart we are required to sing them with uncorrupt and undefiléd tongues. The *Phos Hilaron*, one of the earliest Christian hymns sung at the kindling of lights in the evening, liberates the soul from

[14] Thomas Merton, *Praying the Psalms* (The Liturgical Press, Collegeville, Minnesota, 1956), p. 7.
[15] *Confessions* X, xxxiii, 49-50, translated Pine Coffin.

the fear of the encroaching darkness. The hymn concludes with words which reiterate the importance of singing with integrity:

> Worthy are you at all times to be sung with holy voices,
> O Son of God, O giver of life,
> and to be glorified through all creation.

Perhaps holy voices can also mean whole voices, voices that come from the heart and express the integrity of the heart. Voices that express our whole being and purpose before God, voices that have been sanctified as the sound of the word made flesh within us. These voices don't have to be perfectly tuneful; these voices just have to be true. What would it mean for the church to sing with a whole voice, and with one voice? It is not certain if the contemporary theological direction of the church can allow us to be as optimistic as our forebears were in this ambition. Along with the divisions and factions of the church, largely based on oppositional views on human embodiment and how that embodiment is expressed, we hold on ever more weakly to try and be part of the Body of Christ, a 'communion', but that communion is increasingly one where we cannot even sing together with one voice yet alone share in one bread. We seem to exist in a long night of weeping as the world looks on with scornful wonder at our schisms and irrelevance, and those who long to respond to God's eternal call, continue to wait for the morning of song.[16]

Sacramental Song

As a chorister, the connection between what is sung with the lips, believed in the heart, and shown forth in the life was instilled in me through what is known as the Chorister's

[16]   From the fourth verse of the Hymn 'The Church's one foundation is Jesus Christ her Lord' by Samuel J. Stone (1866).

Prayer.[17] At the end of every choir practice, sat on wooden benches in the vestry, we used to say this prayer together until it was engraved on our hearts. These words acknowledged that singing is a form of embodied prayer and helped the singer reflect positively on the act of incorporating sacred song into the lungs, heart, and mind. The same is true for congregations. A singing church is surely a believing church, and a believing church, is surely a church that sings? The prayer also reminds us of our corporality as worshipping creatures, acknowledging that 'we' do this singing together and that together we minister in the temple as servants of God.

Martin Luther also understood the power of communal singing as part of a faith well lived. Luther suggested that music was able to bear the word of God and the Gospel was preached through the medium of music. Luther's Reformation was attentive to the power of music and specifically sung music to deepen faith and as a minister and musician, he understood the need for congregational singing in worship. He was conscious that the voice expressed the feeling and meaning of words and enabled the words of scripture to become flesh by being expressed through flesh. A more contemporary advocate of congregational singing, John L. Bell, explores why singing is important in his book *The Singing Thing* (2000) and offers that we sing because we are created to sing, but we also sing to make our identity, express emotion, give meaning to words, reflect on the past and shape the future, to tell stories, give of ourselves

[17] The Chorister's Prayer, first published as such in the Choir Boy's Pocket Book (1934): Bless, O Lord, us thy servants, who minister in thy temple. Grant that what we sing with our lips, we may believe in our hearts, and what we believe in our hearts, we may show forth in our lives. Through Jesus Christ our Lord. Amen.

and obey the command which so clearly runs through the scriptures: to sing a new song. Bell suggests that every time a congregation sings it is a one-time offering of praise, because never again will that time, day, place, season, liturgy, congregation be in the same configuration. We sing a new song every time we gather and 'it is important that every song sung is offered to God with that sense of uniqueness. God is worth it.' [18] This is perhaps why we have to keep on singing.

If, as stated in the Westminster Catechism, our chief end as human beings is to glorify God and to enjoy God forever, music and song offer us a means to give God glory through praise and worship; music enables the universal church to sing with one voice and in unison with the church in heaven. In 1588, William Byrd published his *Psalms, Sonnets and Songs*, expressing his 'Reasons to Sing'. These included an acknowledgement that singing was good for health and 'opens the pipes of the singer', and singing was able to help with speech and diction and was part of a good education, but the final reason to sing seems to be the summation of all his other reasons: The better the voice is, William Byrd said, the better ('meeter') it is to honour and serve God therewith: and the voice of man is chiefly to be employed to that end. The purpose of song was to offer praise, which is our ultimate purpose.

In the Sanctus of the Eucharistic prayer, the heavenly song of praise is preceded by the words, 'Therefore, with angels and archangels and all the company of heaven, we laud and magnify your glorious name, for evermore praising you and singing...' and then those words of invitation soon follow: 'Though we are many, we are one body because we all share in one bread'. Could they be re-interpreted thus:

[18]   *The Singing Thing: A Case for Congregational Song*, John L. Bell (Wild Goose Publications, 2000), p. 81.

'Though we are many, we are one body because we all sing with one voice?' If you have ever sung William Byrd's, 'Sanctus from the Four Part Mass', you will understand the profundity of this kind of polyphony, where equal but different voices entwine and embrace and evolve together to combine in their praise of God most high, balanced exquisitely to ensure no voice outshines another, no voice overpowers, but each individual voice is valued, cherished and lifts hearts to heaven. It is a possibility that without this kind of corporate singing, there would be no church and the church is not fully the church if it does not sing together. Dare we suggest that there is something sacramental about the church's song? We could interpret the church's song as an outward and audible symbol of an inward and spiritual grace. When the church sings together, it is a sacrifice of praise, a self-giving act, whereby we put our all on the altar.

Congregational song as a ritual symbol is explored by Judith Marie Kubicki and Jacques Berthier in the context of the music of the Taizé Community in Southern France. The chants of Taizé are much more than a graceful expression of prayer, they are integral to the liturgy itself and to the ministry within it. The songs, as carefully chosen scriptural texts married to simple chants, are signs and symbols of the gathered community and bind people together from across the world in a spirit of peace and reconciliation.[19] There, in something resembling an aircraft hangar in a village near to Cluny, thousands of young people from the corners of the earth gather in prayer, and as grains once dispersed on the hillside are reunited in bread and wine, so they are made into one body through their song of sacrifice and praise.

If forty thousand football fans can turn a game, what could a myriad of voices do when singing in praise of God

[19]   *Liturgical Music as Ritual Symbol, A Case Study of Jacques Berthier's Taizé Music*, Judith Marie Kubicki, Jacques Berthier, Peeters (1999), p. 93.

together? Perhaps this is why I found my experience of chanting in a football stadium quasi-spiritual: I yearned for the church to be something like this in its earthly manifestation. As I stood in the midst of many voices singing together, my own body was resonating with the sound and being moved by the emotion of that experience, but the content of the song meant nothing to me, it was empty praise. The words were frivolous, malicious, jocular. My experiences in Taizé felt like they were verging on the sacramental and were more like the church envisioned by those early Christians; a church which would sing psalms, hymns and spiritual songs together with one voice. The chants, shaped by the scriptures and the simple liturgies holding silence together, bound me with a community made up of people from every continent and island. This was unifying, it was embodied, it was a sign and symbol of that universal catholic church for which I longed.

Can we use the experience of singing together as a framework for our ecclesiologies of the future? Can song become a sacramental action of the church? Why is it so hard for us to sing together with one voice? It could be argued that we have lost something of the vision for the universal church of Christ; we have become so much the local expression of catholicism that we have lost our catholicity, we don't seem to have a common song to sing anymore, and we are reluctant to sing the songs of others. Individualism and subjectivity (and indeed style) in the church's song have usurped the corporate. We have become so specialised and so bespoke, perhaps we have even become so culturally relevant, as to be lost in our sense of corporate and common prayer as our purpose. We now have so many songs that it's difficult to find a song in common. If forty thousand Christians were gathered in a stadium, what would they sing and what could that singing do? Could it turn our game? Perhaps the church needs to go back to basics: the psalms, hymns and spiritual songs of our faith and sing them over and over again until those words are engraved on our hearts. We need to keep on singing these songs until what we sing with our lips, we believe in our hearts, and what we believe in our hearts we show forth in our lives.

CHAPTER FIVE

The Voice of the Church

For bells are the voice of the church;
They have tones that touch and search
The hearts of young and old.
Henry Wadsworth Longfellow, Complete Works (ed. 1883)

It's around eleven o'clock on the thirty-first of December. The city of York is buzzing and excitable as one terrible year begins to fade away into the distance and people tentatively start to feel brave enough to look towards what might lie ahead. Another beginning, another chance. As the world holds its breath in anticipation of midnight, the bells of the cathedral begin to ring out the old year and ring in the new. The tumultuous sounds of chime after chime after chime are pealing through the air and overwhelming the darkness with audible light. They launch into their song, their voices vibrant with a brightening sound, exhilarating and full of hope. They cast their spell over the city and enliven it. They add another dimension to the boozy celebrations and beatify and honour this particular keeping of time. They sing out and seem to preach their message that all things will be made new, and there is no need to be afraid.

In his poem 'Ring out Wild Bells' published in 1850, Alfred Tennyson suggested that the vocation of bells was to ring out the darkness of the land, and 'Ring in the Christ that is to be.'[1] It feels as if that is what the bells are doing tonight and how we need to hear their voice. We need a

---

[1] 'Ring out Wild Bells', the poem published in 1850 by Alfred Lord Tennyson as part of *In Memoriam*. The bells in question were thought to be the bells of Waltham Abbey, heard on New Year's Eve.

new start, and it seems right for them to invoke Christ. In the year being rung out there has been national mourning of a beloved Queen, coming not long after a crippling pandemic. Commentators talk of our need to recover from corporate trauma. There have been three Prime Ministers in the space of three months as our friends in Europe looked upon our political affairs from a distance and wondered what was happening to this great nation. There has been industrial unrest on a scale last seen in the 1970s. The economy has nose-dived into recession, people cannot afford to heat their homes, and families queue for parcels handed out by foodbanks. There is, what has been described as, a tsunami of need; there is homelessness and a growing sense of despondency and un-ease on the streets. The National Health Service and the once envied welfare state are groaning under unprecedented pressure and lack of resource. The old adversaries of racism, misogyny, homophobia, and aggressive nationalism have begun to rear up and creep around the corridors of hard and soft power, their influence becoming normalised in the media without anyone really noticing or objecting. There is a sense of exhaustion everywhere and fear has turned our hearts and souls inwards. Where there is fear, there is also hatred. The gloss of 'everything is fine' is becoming tarnished and we are left with a somehow meaner and harsher reality. There is a sense that we do need to ring something out, and ring in something new. So please let it be Christ that we ring in, imploring him to bring peace, mercy, wisdom and love into this world: ring out wild bells and let this year die.

It was on a New Year's Eve that Lord Peter Wimsey found himself stranded in the Fens of East Anglia and introduced to the bells of Fenchurch St Paul. The kindly Rector informed him that to welcome in the New Year the village band will ring fifteen thousand, eight hundred and forty Kent Treble Bob Majors, a peal lasting over nine hours. Any peal is a worthy ambition for any band of ringers, but it is also a serious test of intellectual and physical stamina. Dorothy L. Sayers suggests that to some listeners, the sound of a peal of bells is like a 'monotonous jangling and nuisance mitigated only by remote distance and sentimental association', but she later goes on to describe the mathematical seriousness of the endeavour as perfect in order, cadence and metre.[2] You could say that a peal is as perfect and as mathematically complete within itself as any Fugue written by J. S. Bach.

At the centre of the plot of *The Nine Tailors*, is the mysterious death of a thief, murderer, and bigamist whose past crimes are uncovered amongst the villagers of Fenchurch St Paul just before the New Year's Eve celebrations. He is temporarily tied up in the bell chamber while they decide how to handle his deception and dastardliness. Quite unexpectedly, he is found dead two days later and then to protect and deceive, his body is mutilated and buried. Wimsey is called back to investigate a few months later when the body is discovered and naturally all becomes clear, but the mystery remains as to the cause of death of this master criminal. Wimsey returns to Fenchurch the following Christmas when the bells are rung again in urgent warning as the sluice fails and the flood waters rise across the Fens. Sayers uses the voice of the bells to warn the world of an impending judgement. As the bells raise the alarm, the detective comes to the realisation that these bells can sound death as well as life. He finds himself in the bell chamber and the sound is frightful and the bells are a violent assault on the mind, body, and spirit. Being exposed to the awesome and terrible sound of the bells for hour upon hour on that fateful New Year's Eve, would be enough to kill a

[2] Dorothy L. Sayers, *The Nine Tailors*, p. 20.

man, concludes Wimsey. Justice appears to have been done. Judgement comes with the flood.

As a whodunnit, the identity of the person or persons who killed the crook is rather disappointing, the eight Bells of Fenchurch St Paul seem to hold the secret: Gaude, Sabaoth, John, Jericho, Jubilee, Dimitry, Batty Thomas and Tailor Paul, and they were beyond any judgement because they were already hanged. It is tempting to consider whether Sayers, a theologian in her own right, is offering the bell as a theological cipher, a latent symbol of the faith, a fearless messenger, and a sign of good overcoming evil. The voice of the bell is not simply sweetness and light, it is the jangling sound of Christ casting out demons and menacing the devil. Sayers seems to be suggesting that the sound of good found in the voice of these noble bells can overwhelm, and exorcise the evil in their midst, drowning out and deafening the greed, the hatred, the sin and the strife of humanity and ringing out darkness from the land, trampling down death by death. This vocation of the bell has historical precedent: in the Venice of the fourteenth century, the bells which had been birthed by the bronze forges of that city were exorcised, washed, anointed and blessed by Bishops. The bishop prayed that through their voice the snares of the devil may be ineffectual, the wind and waters calmed, the air be free from disease and plague and the darkness might flee away when it heard the sweeter music of their song. [3]

The Defiance of Bells

Wherever there are bells they will ring as an outward and audible sign and symbol of a deeper grace. The bells of chapels, churches and cathedrals most obviously speak for the church into our time and into our lives, they are part

[3]   Victoria Avery, *Vulcan's Forge in Venus City, The Story of Bronze in Venice, 1350-1650* (Oxford University Press, 2011).

of the soundtrack of Anglicanism and across the nation the sound of bells offers a kind of stability, a kind of nostalgia and a sense of continuity in an age of incredible change. Even if you do not believe, even if you do not pray, these bells are still for you, reminding you that the God you don't believe in loves you. It must be somehow reassuring to know that when bells ring, prayers are being said by others, vicariously: for you and for everyone.

Upon the death of Queen Elizabeth II, the bells of the nation had a sombre message to share, the sound of a fully muffled peal of church bells was heard across the nation for the first time in over seventy years. This particular form of ringing is reserved for the death of a monarch and this ethereal sound was last heard upon the death of George VI. The muffled peal sounded as if it was coming from another time and place. This solemn tintinnabulation evoked feelings of remoteness and distance almost as if it was coming to us from underwater - from a submerged and ghostly cathedral; over the top of this spectral peal of bells was a lone un-muffled tenor bell tolling in the present, a toll for each year of her life, lamenting with each strike, and offering a prayer to send a forth a Christian soul upon her journey.

As part of their daily life, these bells also mark the passing of time not in years but in hours and minutes. When not powered by many hands and huge physical effort they are often mechanised. In this place they ring out every fifteen minutes, building up to their hourly chime which sings out the tune of 'York', a common metre metrical hymn which takes as its partner a form of words from Psalm 122: *'Pray that Jerusalem may have, peace and felicity'*. In the autumn of 2023, this song was sung as the Holy Land once again became a place of bloody conflict.

Over the city, within and beyond its walls these bells sing of peace and prosperity, day after day after day. The very thought that the words of a psalm, articulating the hope and peace of Christ, are being rung out and sung out over this city is a comfort in such a fractious and divided society but also a subversion of it. I would be fearful of what would happen in our world if they did not ring, or if they were not there at all. It's unlikely that many make these connections, but the church knows what it is doing, and the bells have a clear evangelistic purpose. Through their witness the message is shared, the seed has been scattered, who knows where and how it will land. Through her bells the church is witnessing to greater truths and somehow providing space for the Christian imagination to flower, reminding the world that there is another story to tell.

The Bells are the voice of the church, so said Henry Wadsworth Longfellow. From stone edifices, from belfries and from towers, the bells of the church preach and pray, their song of peace and love drifting over towns and cities and creating a soundscape into which the message of their maker and redeemer falls softly like snow upon the ears, touching the hearts of young and old. Bells are vocational creations, semi-animate. They are born from the depths of the earth with fire and then they are 'baptised'. Liturgies are created for their blessing and dedication, and within those liturgies, prayers are made that their voices may be heard and that their voice may direct ours to God. The liturgies also express that the purpose of the bell is to bind the church together as one voice, in fellowship and friendship. Bells are named and commissioned for their great calling; they are far from utilitarian. They witness to so much more than the prettifying of a city's soundscape. They are preaching, they sound out a public proclamation. The bell is the most obvious and possibly the most mystical way in which the church speaks, one of the few signs of the church that audibly moves beyond its own walls and into the communities which it serves.

From their pulpit, they mark out our time as God's time, they call the faithful to worship, they remember the dead and celebrate love, they give warning, they lament, they rejoice with those who rejoice and weep with those who weep. They give voice to the reality of the word made flesh, the Christ that is to be. They are sounding out the reality of love made real, they are sounding out the reality of the life, death and resurrection of Christ on the high street, at the war memorial, in the clinic, at the hostel, along the riverside, around the city walls, in the market place, in the job centre, in the bars, restaurants and museums; they are a symbol of the church speaking into the public square, they are a sign of Christ's presence. In a church which increasingly struggles to make its voice heard, her sweet chiming bells are determined in their message, they remind the Christian of their vocation to speak into society and culture with confidence and without shame. Defiantly. Courageously.

The Gospel-song of the bells cannot alone solve the problems of society or heal its dis-ease, but this song can impart a message to listening ears and eager hands and hearts so that everyone touched by this message can indeed change the world for the better. The Gospel-song of the bells cannot speak into the specific complexities of unemployment or recession or poverty, but their music can provide a space for the imagination to expand and the message of justice and love to be articulated over all. A simple message of justice and love does have something to say to a world beset with inequality, division and selfishness. So, in a symbolic and mystical sense, the bells are able to lift our vision and raise the aspirations of society towards the good, appealing to our better selves, made in the image of God.

There has long been debate and disagreement as to how the church should speak into contemporary society and use its voice to reflect on the social ordering of our world.

In essence the relationship between the ecclesial realm and political realm has always been fraught with tension, even Christ himself was incited to respond to those who asked him to whom taxes should be paid, God or Caesar? Bishops have long been told to keep out of politics and be silent on the issues that affect us all. This kind of castigation and silencing reached a new peak when a Conservative MP called on Church of England Bishops to stop 'preaching from the pulpit' as they responded to a government decision to send refugees to processing centres in Rwanda.[4] Earlier in the same year, the Archbishop of Canterbury in his Easter Day Sermon, had challenged this course of action as undermining the Christian values of British society, and extolled instead the virtues of mercy, justice and love in the light of the resurrection.[5] Telling the church not to preach from its own pulpits, is like telling a bell not to ring.

William Temple, in Christianity and Social Order, reflected on the role of the church in society at a time when a post-war United Kingdom was beset by social problems: unemployment, poverty, a housing shortage, vulnerability among the communities of the elderly, sick and disabled and inadequate educational and health provision. There was a great deal that needed healing. The deeper societal problems were identified and named in the Beveridge Report of 1942 as want, disease, ignorance, squalor and idleness. Temple, speaking from a theological position expounded the virtues of justice and love, and created space for a vision which was generous enough to provide a Christian architectonic for the practical outworking of a new welfare state.

[4] https://www.theguardian.com/commentisfree/2022/dec/23/the-guardian-view-on-pulpit-politics-not-just-for-christmas
[5] https://www.archbishopofcanterbury.org/speaking-writing/sermons/archbishop-justins-sermon-easter-day-holy-communion-canterbury-cathedral

Temple was quick to state that the church was seldom tasked with, or indeed capable of, solving all the practical problems found in society, that was largely the work of the instruments of government, but it could voice, or ring out, the principles of freedom, fellowship and service to which, from a Christian perspective, every good society should aspire. In essence, Temple was also creating a space for the Christian imagination so as to 'lift the parties to a level of thought and feeling at which the problem disappears'.[6] The voice of the church, like the sounding of her bells, could create a realm through which a Christian interpretation of the world could be reached, or at least the means of being able to reach it. The voice of the church will always be in the world but not of the world, ringing in the possibility of a different kind of kingdom.

A naïve reading of the vocation of bells, sees them as harmless heritage adornments to the cultural sound world of a city or society. The church and her message is judged in a similar way, as something on the edge of society, a pretty distraction, benign and largely irrelevant. How wrong this assumption is on both counts. The bell, as a symbol of the voice of the church is commissioned to sing her song of subversion and salvation to a world in need of God and remain undaunted in that vocation. We must never underestimate the power of that song and the need for imaginative spaces to articulate what the world is called to be in Christ.

In 1969, Michael Ramsey climbed the bell tower of Canterbury Cathedral to toll the bell one hundred and fifty times as a call for peace in Nigeria as the Biafran War raged on; the tolling bell was also a lament over the innocent lives that had been lost. On 3 March 2022 the cathedral bells of

---

6   William Temple, *Christianity and Social Order*, p. 43.

Europe rang out in solidarity with the people of Ukraine as they endured Russian invasion - the peal was offered as a prayer and as an invocation of peace. On 30 October 2022, bells across the Church of England rang out on the Eve of the United Nations Climate Conference in Glasgow, calling the world to account for the abuse and degradation of creation and as a warning of the growing climate crisis. These bells rang out as both an appeal to the conscience and heart of society and as a petition for global justice. Even the church needed to hear this message as it continued to invest in fossil fuels and benefit from those dividends. The bells of the church still ring out in challenge, their voice harnessed as an urgent alarm against evil and sin, pricking consciences in anticipation of coming judgement, reminding the church what it is for.

Angels' Song

Again, if the Bell is the voice of the church, their ringing is a sign and symbol of the church's vocation to name those things which comfortable society may wish to ignore, to sound out against injustice and warn against complacency. The bells give warning of our adversary the devil, prowling around and flexing his muscles. The vocation of the church is to sing out Christ and his Gospel over and above the pettiness of our politics and the self-serving ambitions of our broken humanity. The bells keep us alert and awake somewhere between the now and the not yet. Without so much as a word, the bells speak loudly and clearly again and again of the peace that Christ will bring if people are ready to hear.

In the Christmas carol, 'It came upon the midnight clear', the angels of heaven sing of that same much needed peace. They hover over the earth and their heavenly music floats over the weary world, their music dulls the babel-sounds that are voiced from the self-centred and the proud who think they are gods. The angels sing a love-song to humanity: their message is peace over strife, love over hate, they call on the world to hush and listen to their music as the Christ child is born; they provide a space for the people of this planet to imagine for themselves another narrative. At the end of time, when all are things are reconciled, the earth will return to God the love-song which they have shared. It is somewhere in this realm of angels' song that the voice of the bell is also heard, an echo of their message in the present, a symbol of angels hovering overhead willing an end to all need, sorrow, and confusion and dispelling the evil in their midst. At the very same time, this music is like the first green shoot emerging from winter, a first sounding of the love-song we are called to return to our maker.

The Angelus, is of course, the angel bell. The bell that recalls the incarnation of Christ and is so named after the message of the angel to the Virgin Mary: *Hail Mary, full of grace, the Lord is with thee: Blessed art thou among women, and blessed is the fruit of thy womb Jesus. Holy Mary, Mother of God, pray for us sinners, now and at the hour of our death.* Traditionally, the Angelus bell is rung three times a day: at its beginning, at noon and at eventide, and the bells that were called to ring out the Angelus were often named after the angel messenger, Gabriel. The ringing of this bell was a sign and symbol of Christ's incarnation encroaching on daily life, reminding the faithful and unfaithful alike that God was with them, wherever they were, in the fields or at home, experiencing moments of distress or times of jubilation. There was no time or place where the angels' song could not be heard, there was no place Christ would not go.

In the painting *Angelus*, by the French artist Jean-François Millet (1857–1859), a peasant man and peasant woman stand in a field, they have obviously been digging for what looks like potatoes, and it appears they haven't found many. In the distance on the horizon, is the church tower and the suggestion is that the Angelus has just been rung, presumably at midday. The man has taken off his hat, has lain up his fork and is standing still, head bowed. The woman bows her head and clasps her hands in prayer. Daily life is paused for a minute as the sound of the angelus intrudes upon their earthly activity. The voice of this bell takes them away, for just a moment, from the struggles of the present and though their heads are bowed down to the mud and dirt beneath them, their hearts and souls are raised to heaven.

In many parts of the world the Angelus is still sounded today, in schools and hospitals, in villages and towns, on the radio and even as an App on Google Play. The bell is still shaping time and space, and as a symbol of the church proclaims the constant presence of the Body of Christ in the world, the sound of unceasing prayer. The bleeding of holy sounds into daily life is a gift for all ears, for those who choose to hear and those who refuse, for the sacred and for the secular. This proclamation, ringing out loudly and clearly and with no shame whatsoever, is equally shared, an indiscriminate and eternal message of love.

The power of the bell is in its persistence. The ringing bell is almost a defiance. Their voice is an incursion of the spiritual on the temporal, and of the theological upon the secular. Their sound speaks for the unheard, the forgotten, the lonely, the sick, the dying, and it speaks of the love, mercy, kindness, and healing power of Christ, whose song could never be destroyed. They sing of the dance that will never die, they sing 'Gloria in excelsis' in the face of human sin and death. When our world descends into chaos, and our societies fracture, when we descend into despondency and lose hope, we are called to listen to the angels' song which enables us to imagine other futures of peace and felicity.

When the church is told to be quiet, she should preach even more loudly to remind everyone of their humanity and the causes of justice and love to which we are, at our best, called to embody. When the church is ignored and mocked and side-lined as irrelevant, it is called to devotion, daily and hourly as the angelus sweetly reminds us, and to defiantly keep on praying and never lose heart. The church is also called to use its voice and speak out, as raucous and as arresting as a peal of bells tumbling out over a city: subversive, courageous, faithful, a monotonous jangling and a nuisance if need be, reminding the world that there is another story to tell.

CHAPTER SIX

A Humble Voice

'Worship, then, at every level, always means God
and the priority of God'
Evelyn Underhill, Worship (1936)

On Easter Day, 2021, the Grand Organ of York Minster was brought back to life after a once in a century refurbishment. The liturgy for the waking-up of the instrument after its lengthy slumber, incorporated elements from a Roman Catholic liturgy for the Benediction of the *Grandes-Orgues de l'Église Notre Dame de Vimoutiers* in 2019 alongside prayers from the dedication service of the previous re-incarnation of the Minster organ upon its dedication in 1903. There were various invocations calling upon the organ to sing itself back into life: 'Awake, O Sacred instrument' said a voice, 'Sing of Jesus, our Lord, dead and risen for us today'; the organist responded with a glorious improvisation to each bidding. 'Awake, O Sacred instrument' said another voice, 'Bring the congregation of the faithful together in songs of thanksgiving and praise'.

It was beautiful to orchestrate a once in a life-time liturgy and observe this instrument re-take its place at the heart of the worshipping church. It was as if it was returning to its sole vocation and reclaiming the purpose which gave it meaning. As I reflected on this auspicious day, it struck me that its dedication and re-birth were somehow articulating the human vocation to worship and praise, here was an instrument made of wood and metal embodying our ultimate purpose before God.

The prayers mined from the 1903 liturgy were sobering. They were the kind of prayers we rarely hear these days which made me want to use them even more. There was a solemnity about these words which seemed to rightly order and orientate the worship of the church away from pride and ego and towards our transcendent other. These prayers were directional, they were to and for God. As Evelyn Underhill describes, they were the response of the creature to the Eternal.[1] These prayers reminded everyone that worship only ever has one purpose, it is neither for self nor for society, though of course the benefits of worship inform both and help both to flourish; it is neither an education nor an entertainment, worship should give glory to God alone. These prayers used at a similar occasion over a century before were unashamed in this assertion.

It was perhaps paradoxical that such prayers were written to dedicate an instrument of such magnitude, such reputation and such grandeur, and an instrument which required such skill to play. Pomp could easily have reared its ugly head, but not so here. These were prayers of perspective and for the tempering of human pride. These prayers reminded us all, clergy, musicians, congregation, that we were all creatures of the creator, and not worthy even gather up the crumbs from under the table, but there we were nonetheless, honoured guests at the banquet.

How we need these kinds of prayers today when it is so easy to think that the human being is the ultimate focus of our worship, how hard it is to give ourselves to God and offer the kind of worship which is beyond 'churchy' concerns and instead taps into eternity. These were the kind of prayers

---

[1]   Evelyn Underhill, *Worship*, The Nature of Worship (1936), Chapter 1, p. 3.

which called upon worshippers to come before the Lord with a pure heart and humble voice, unto the throne of the heavenly grace (those words from the penitential introduction to the Evening Service of the Book of Common Prayer) and reminded everyone whose praise was being offered.

> Almighty Father, who hast filled thy servants with the Spirit of God, in wisdom and in understanding, and in all manner of workmanship to devise instruments of music, to be used in the worship of thy sanctuary. Be pleased to prosper the use of this renovated organ which we now dedicate to thy service in this thy hallowed house of prayer.
>
> Grant that it may tend to the promotion of thy glory and the edification of thy people. Grant that all to whom thou hast given skill in music and song, may ever seek to set forth thy praise, not their own, and to lift up the hearts and minds of those who hear them, not to themselves but to thee. Grant that all who worship here, even if they sing not with their voices, may join in the songs of praise with the spirit and understanding, and thus be united with all who stand before thee on earth or in heaven in offering to thee the worship of spirit and truth. Amen. [2]

Finding a voice

The musical resurrection on Easter Day could not come soon enough, and for me and for many others, it became a localised symbol of renewed hope in a time of global despair. The Grand Organ had not been heard in the Minster since

[2]   From 'Evensong for Easter Day with the Dedication of the Grand Organ' Sunday 4 April 2021, York Minster, and the 'Service for the Re-construction and Dedication of the Screen Organ in York Minster', during Easter Week, 15 April 1903, by permission of the Chapter of York.

2018 and this silence was exacerbated by the global pandemic of 2020 which thwarted communal worship by closing the doors of our churches and cathedrals and disrupting the functioning of society itself by winding down every kind of business, office and school. A careful and cautious approach meant this enforced lull in the usually frenetic activity of this cathedral could be taken advantage of, and presented the organ builders with unprecedented access, time, and space to reconstruct and re-voice this mighty organ by day and by night.

Given all the challenges which had to be overcome during this plague year, when this mighty organ re-sounded to herald the risen Christ, one could not help seeing this rejuvenated instrument as a sign of a new beginning after months of being in, what had felt like, a perpetual lent. The Grand Organ had somehow taken upon itself the mantle of magic and myth, sign and wonder and like a phoenix from the flames it roared through the Easter Day liturgies and sang for a congregation who were not permitted to sing for fear of an invisible airborne virus.

In the face of such an atomised enemy, it gave voice to the fragmented community of the faithful who had been quietened for too long behind screens and surgical masks, and behind those same masks on that day when the organ found its voice, there were tears of joy because something that had been lost had suddenly been found, and that which was dead had suddenly come to life.

The refurbishment of an iconic instrument such as this is a once in a century event. The whole deconstruction and subsequent reconstruction were fastidiously documented, and the planning of the project stretched back at least a decade involving hundreds of people. The scaffolding required for the dismantling and rebuilding was a feat of engineering and not one thing was left to chance, even the font used to inscribe each of the stops was chosen and designed with care. I suppose it was a little like building the first computer or the engine of a huge ship: as challenging physically as it was technically. But unlike a computer, this machine seemed to have a soul, or at least be *soulful*, and its seat was in the heart of a building created to give praise to Almighty God. The vocation of this instrument was bound up with the vocation and purpose of the church itself.

More than five thousand individual pipes had to be cleaned, repaired and made new in the workshop of Harrison and Harrison Organ Builders in Durham, and the mechanics and acoustic engineering of this particular instrument, situated in this particular space, were re-examined and re-imagined for the twenty first century. The last time that such a mammoth task had been undertaken was when Edward VII was King, Arthur Balfour was Prime Minister and Thomas Tertius Noble was the Organist of York Minster. This was the year when the Wright Brothers' 'Flyer' performed its first manned flight and Emmeline Pankhurst founded the Suffrage movement with the Women's Social and Political Union. The first decade of the twentieth century was a time of optimism and ambition, it was the decade of art nouveau, the internal combustion engine, it was the decade in which Einstein published his special theory of relativity and the soundtrack included Debussy, Mahler, Rachmaninoff and Strauss, all pushing musical boundaries in their different ways.

The 1903 organ also witnessed the twentieth century unfold with its world wars, global pandemics (not unlike the one we were living through), economic depressions and natural disasters of flood, famine and storm. It also looked on as the community of York buried their dead, were joined together in holy matrimony and gave thanks for the birth of a child. Day by day, it performed its bread-and-butter duties and lived into its vocation as it accompanied the songs and prayers of the faithful.

On Monday 6 August 1945, on the Feast of the Transfiguration, an atomic bomb was dropped on the city of Hiroshima. The Minster Organ was playing 'Ireland in C' and the choir sang 'I sat down under his Shadow' by Sir Edward Bairstow at the Eucharist. In 1984, lightning struck, and the organ coughed, spluttered and breathed in too much smoke as fire ravaged the south transept roof. Thankfully, it survived. On 30 November 2005, the Minster Organ offered fanfares alongside African drummers as Britain's first Black Archbishop was enthroned and in 2015 it sang out as the first woman was ordained a Bishop in the Church of England in York Minster. What changes and chances would this new instrument observe in this fleeting world as the decades rolled on? In a hundred years from now, where might we be? What kind of church would it preside over in the twenty-first century?

Set apart

The 1903 instrument was witness to the already declining church; the church of the Edwardian era was often blind to the ebbing away of the faithful and the secularization of society and rather than facing the music it often responded by being more zealous and building more churches. Like the church in every age it held together the paradox of unbridled optimism with an often unspoken and fearful pessimism.[3] Since the 1851 Census of Religious Worship, the decline in religious affiliation has gone from more than half the adult population attending worship on any given to Sunday to less

---

[3]   S. J. D. Green, *Religion in the Age of Decline: Organisation and Experience in Industrial Yorkshire, 1870-1920* (Cambridge University Press, 1996), 381.

than one twelfth by the end of the twentieth century.[4] In the twenty years since, the decline has continued and rapidly accelerated. As the plans were being made concrete for the refurbishment of the Minster organ and the fundraising continued in earnest, the 2019 census data from the Church of England revealed that less than 1 per cent of the population attended church regularly.[5] The census in 2021 would reveal that only 46.2 per cent of the population called themselves Christian, but of that number few practised, making Christianity a minority religion.

What was the point of spending all that money (nearly two million pounds) on an instrument for a dying church? It is a legitimate question in a world and a church driven by economics, utility, and statistics for growth, but the Grand Organ of York Minster, like the building of which it is part, serves a different purpose which is perhaps beyond utility, beyond strategy, beyond economics and ultimately beyond price. Rightly or wrongly, the church often measures its 'success' by the number of those who worship, as if numbers mean everything. With an air of unbridled optimism, the Church of England of 2021 proclaimed that over the next ten years, 10,000 new Christian communities would be created. The restoration of the Grand Organ of York Minster was asserting that even if numbers continued to decline, the worship of God and the music which enlivened that worship would be at the heart of what this particular church considered 'worth it' and its central purpose for the next one hundred years.

The words of the modern-day Saint and Martyr, Oscar

[4] Crockett, A., and Voas, D. (2006), 'Generations of Decline: Religious Change in 20th-Century Britain', *Journal for the Scientific Study of Religion*, 45(4), 567–584. http://www.jstor.org/stable/4621936

[5] https://www.churchofengland.org/sites/default/files/2020-10/2019StatisticsForMission.pdf

Romero, who was assassinated when saying Mass on 24 March 1980, are very hard for the economic era church to hear. In his book *The Violence of Love*, he willed us not to measure the church by the number of its members but by the sincerity of heart with which we follow the truth and light of the divine redeemer.[6] Of course, measuring the sincerity of the heart is a near impossible task and who would dare to look into another man's soul? But perhaps Romero's words can help refocus our minds on the intentions of the heart and the simple truth that only two or three need gather in the name of Christ to be the church of Christ and a mighty organ playing for God alone in a near-empty cathedral is good enough for God.

It is from this worship that all else comes: service, mission, evangelisation, justice, community. Without worship and prayer at the heart of the church, the church is nothing and means nothing. Is this justification enough for placing worship at the heart of what the church is called to be and do? If nothing else, our churches and chapels and cathedrals are designated spaces, purposeful spaces, hallowed spaces to focus the prayers and praises of the Christian community. Perhaps an angel weeps and the devil laughs every time a church is de-consecrated and turned into a pub, post-office or swish mezzanine apartment with period Gothic features. This is not said in naivety about the cost and effort of keeping physical buildings in good order, nor indeed the instruments and furnishings which adorn them, but there is cost, and there is *cost*. Whether built through hubris or need, these buildings are signs, concrete (or sandstone) realities of the presence of God in a society which wants to forget God, or only let an unthreatening God out of the box on special occasions.

6   Oscar Romero, *The Violence of Love*, compiled and translated by James R. Brockman SJ (Orbis Books, 2004).

On Voice

In his book *Liturgy and Society*, the Kelham Monk, A G Hebert speaks of the importance of being set apart in God's service through worship. The church building, he says, stands as God's House, not to be exclusively God's House but as a reminder that all the earth is the Lord's and to sanctify every other house and home. So it is with the Lord's Day, set apart so that all time might be known as belonging to God. So with the clergy, designated for the people whom they serve, and so with the use of common things of daily life in prayer and praise, bread, wine and water, and when we read and sing and move, all these activities redeem the corresponding actions in daily life and embrace life in all of its fullness for Christ.[7]

The blessing and dedication of this grand musical instrument in a grand cathedral felt like a message, a symbol of something profound which was hard to articulate at the time. As the church was getting smaller here was a statement of hope about its ultimate purpose. Here was something being set aside for worship alone. The Grand Organ spoke like a heavenly chorus made up of thousands of diverse voices ranging from the tiniest voice spoken through a pipe no bigger than a 3B pencil, to a voice which sounded from a pipe which would not be out of place on the largest ocean liner. This chorus of many voices seemed to gather up in its song the voice of all who heard it, voices which could barely articulate their own hopes, sorrows, fears, and joys, and despite its grandeur it seemed to point beyond itself and speak with humility and nobility, fulfilling its vocation to enable the faithful to speak to God.

One of the many technical feats of the new instrument meant that it projected its voice fully into the nave of the

[7]   A. G. Hebert, *Liturgy and Society: The Function of the Church in the Modern World* (Faber and Faber, London, 1935), 'The Incarnation and Social Life', pp. 191-2.

Cathedral. In terms of engineering and magnitude, many cathedrals face the challenge of instruments which don't quite inhabit the spaces they are called to enliven, but with some switches, shutter work and attention to wind pressures resulting in a much greater 'lung capacity', the York instrument of 2021 is able to reach to the back of the nave and support the singing of thousands. When it speaks it causes you to tremble, it stirs you in the pit of your stomach, it reaches into your soul and drags out emotion. The new instrument has been described as having 'limitless bravura'; it gives completely of itself and then just when you think it has given everything, it gives more, it dares more, it risks more. It always takes you beyond. In contrast, and equally as moving is the ability of the instrument to hold the space with near silence. The quietest stop, the *Echo Dulciana* is like a thread of silk into which any diminuendo can find its way into prayerful stillness. At the end of Herbert Howells' Gloucester Service, this stop is the last voice to be heard, fading into nothing and disappearing into the heavenly realm. Breath-taking. When Eric Milner-White heard the Gloucester Service in York Minster for the first time he said that the experience went beyond the liturgical to the spiritual, and the Nunc Dimittis left him with inward tears for the rest of the day. [8]

The destiny of this instrument, born again on Easter Day 2021, was not to simply sound out the vestiges of Christianity in an empty sepulchre, or provide the background music to a world-famous visitor attraction. The destiny of this instrument was to assert the faith of the church with limitless bravura and continue to be a sign of humanities first calling, which is to worship God and love God forever.[9]

---

[8]   From the Footnotes, Paul Andrews (2012), 'Howells Requiem', Choir of Trinity College Cambridge, Stephen Layton, Hyperion Records.

[9]   From The Westminster Catechism (1647): 'Man's chief end is to glorify God, and to enjoy him forever.'

Its dedication and setting apart was somehow able to redeem all singing and speaking and inspire and liberate all voices to offer praise. The resonance of this instrument was somehow reminding the church what it was for.

Tuned for Praise

It would be easy to think of the organ as being a child of the industrial revolution, a modern musical machine as much a feat of engineering as the steam locomotive, but these instruments have their origins in the ancient world. The Roman water organ or *hydraulis* was the forebear, invented by Ctesibius of Alexandria in around the third century before Christ's birth. The *hydraulis*, as the name suggests, was powered by water and it was able to offer an impressive dynamic range through its various pipes with virtuosic performers enchanting the listener and being at the heart of Roman entertainments, banquets, pagan rites, and theatre. [10] The first organs really did provide the backing track to secular life.

At, or around the time of Christ, the *megrepha*, a primitive and very loud pipe organ was used to call priests and people to worship in the synagogue but the first Christian communities tended to avoid such instruments and instead offered their praises with the voice alone. [11] For centuries the church was suspicious and resistant to instrumentation in worship which was always a *cappella*, or for voice only, but nevertheless, the organ seemed to be accepted at a fairly early stage as an instrument of the establishment, being

[10] Claudian writes of the proto-organist: '*him too whose light touch can elicit loud music from those pipes of bronze that sound a thousand diverse notes beneath his wandering fingers and who by means of a lever stirs to song the labouring water.*' Panegyric on the Consulship of Fl. Manlius Theodorus (A.D. 399).

[11] Paul Westermeyer, *Te Deum, The Church and Music* (Fortress Press, Minneapolis, 1998), p. 21.

Nero's favourite musical instrument. Over time, the pipe organ was found to be a suitable enabler of the church's song to the extent that when one thinks of church worship today, one usually thinks of a 'church organ'. The organ eventually found itself at the heart of Christian worship, most likely through the monasteries and cathedrals of Western Europe. It has become an instrument, a tool, an *organum* of the Christian faith.[12]

To the south of the Grand Organ in York Minster, tucked into a niche just above the south quire aisle is a stone statue of St Cecilia playing a small hand-held organ which she cradles in her arms like a child. I couldn't help looking to the patron saint of organs, musicians, poets, and hymns on the day when the organ sang again. According to 'tradition', Cecilia sang with all her heart at her own wedding, at which she committed herself to remain a perpetual virgin. She is then credited with converting her new husband and his brother to Christianity, with the help of an angelic vision. She was martyred, and again, according to what we might call the legend of St Cecilia, she was put in a bath of fire and yet remained untouched by the flames. It then took three attempts to kill her by the sword. With her head severed she remained alive for three days, preaching and converting many to the faith. Her body is said to have been exhumed in the sixteenth century and found to be un-corrupt and smelling of sweet flowers.

One notable reference to this story is found in The Second Nun's Tale of Chaucer's Canterbury Tales, but there were many other re-tellings which were equally fanciful and became prevalent as a form of pious romance. Saintly women were often pledged in love to God alone, even if they were married, to somehow vanquish the transgression

---

[12]   The Latin term, *Organum* is derived from the Greek 'Organon' meaning instrument, tool or organ.

of Eve with which they were stained, so becoming bright lights to lift mortal vision. This is the St Cecilia for whom odes were written, this is the stylized Cecilia who has been portrayed in art and music as chaste and ethereal, a translator of the songs of heaven for mortal ears, and an example of dedication to God.

Like many other early Saints, there is actually very little to say about the real Cecilia, other than she was probably a Roman Noblewomen who allowed Christians to meet in her home and led a church within it. And therein lies the probable reason for her martyrdom in about the year 230. Her dedication to God would have been seen as a threat to, and a subversion of, the expected dedication of Roman citizens to the state, and her gender and status within the life of the early church a threat to the convention of those who were permitted to have a voice in society. Other legends say that Cecilia was a powerful preacher and converted hundreds of people to Christianity. If this is true, it is easier to understand why the authorities were fearful of a woman who spoke with authority and power on the street corners, in the market place, and in the home.

A church was established on the site of her house in Trastevere, Rome and she became one of the most revered martyrs of the Roman Church; one of only seven women in addition to the Virgin Mary, remembered in the Canon of the Mass. Taken together, the snippets of her hagiography suggest she sang publicly, she spoke publicly and she gathered Christians for public worship, the worship of God being her first true love. Being born into a wealthy Roman family, it is not such a leap to imagine that Cecilia was familiar with the organ. Maybe there was a hydraulis in the corner of her home, maybe she played it on occasion to entertain her father's important guests, as ladies in the eighteenth century played the pianoforte to entertain and entice a prospective beau.

Cecilia was converted to Christianity, we know not how, and expressed her faith through song, which is one of the most public ways of expressing faith, as noisy as it might be beautiful. Like every other woman of the time, she was pledged in marriage by her parents to a well-meaning Roman. At her wedding, which we might surmise was a secular affair, the organ may well have played as it did at important civic occasions, but in protest at her fate, and in opposition to the profane music that was offered, she sang in her heart to the Lord, so re-orientating these instruments of the state to instruments for the worship of God, sanctifying the music and setting it apart for divine glory.

If the human voice is the instrument from which all other instruments come, there must surely be something of the human spirit and the human voice within every musical instrument when played. A musical instrument as the bearer of music is somehow an extension of the self, an articulation of the soul, a means of communicating without words. Musical instruments have always been taken up to express joy, praise and triumph, as described in Psalm 150, but they have also been put down in lament and sorrow, and silenced when there is nothing left to say. To play a musical instrument is also to be taken away from the self, to give of the self completely and to hear a musical instrument can transport the listener and evoke the same response.

Alexander Pope writes in praise of Cecilia in his 'Ode on St Cecilia's Day' and concludes his verse by praising music and the instruments that make it, as intermediaries between humanity and God and 'when the full organ joins the tuneful quire th'immortal powers incline their ear'. John Dryden, in the sixth stanza of his 'Song for St Cecilia's Day' (1687) goes even further in his Ode suggesting that the voice of the organ surpasses even the human voice in inspiring holy love. In the 'Anthem for St Cecilia's Day' (1940), famously set to music by Benjamin Britten, W. H. Auden notes that *'this innocent virgin constructed an organ to enlarge her prayer and notes tremendous from her great engine thundered out on the Roman air.'* Despite the romance of St Cecilia and her standing as a muse for wistful poetry, there is a hint of an idea running through her legend suggesting that she was someone who made a noise. No meek and mild deportment, no quiet virgin. Her body, her soul and her voice were tuned for praise and proclamation and yet the telling and re-telling of her story over time gradually and subtly silenced the real Cecilia as ably as her persecutors. The myth of St Cecilia and the silencing of her voice within it, is as troubling as her martyrdom. Here is woman of faith, dedicated to God who has been sanctified and set apart by a church which simultaneously, over the centuries silenced her sisters from singing, from playing music and from speaking within it. This is perhaps why, when I sang 'O Lord, open thou our lips' and preached from the pulpit of York Minster on Easter Day accompanied by a newly dedicated organ, I hoped St Cecilia might be looking on with joy.

J. S. Bach understood very well, perhaps as St Cecilia did, that music is made to the glory of God alone; he would sign his music *Soli Deo Gloria*, to signify who and what the music was for. Only when we orient our voices aright and sign our lives with the words, *to the glory of God alone*, can we be truly humble.

CHAPTER SEVEN

Voices and their Bodies

Voice is a kind of sound characteristic of what has soul in it;
nothing that is without soul utters voice.
Aristotle, *De Anima* (384-322BC)

In his work *De Anima*, Aristotle suggests that the voice of animate beings are an echo of the soul, or a window into it. Musical instruments like the harp and lyre, and indeed the organ, emit something of the likeness of the sound of a voice, a similitude of the voice, but the human voice is a direct window into the soul itself.[1] Although we might ascribe 'being' or human likeness to those inanimate things that 'speak', things like bells, and church organs, or musical instruments, their speaking is only enabled by the human hands and hearts and souls that enliven them and invest in making the inanimate, animate; breathing the breath of life into that which is lifeless. It is the voice of the violinist that is channelled through their violin. It is their heart which interprets the black dots and lines on a page into something meaningful, it is their soul that turns this instrument of shaped wood, taut strings, and horsehair into something which connects to the hearts and souls of those who listen.

If we consider the human body as an instrument, our voice is an expression of our own physical and embodied reality and can audibly carry our feelings and emotions. The tone of our spoken voice can give away the thoughts of our hearts and the character of the voice can disclose our age and

[1] Aristotle, *De Anima: The Complete Works of Aristotle*, The Revised Oxford Translation, ed. Jonathan Barnes (Princeton UP, 1984).

gender and reveal the identities and emotions of our deepest selves. The sound of our voice is intimately connected to our bodies, fearfully and wonderfully made, and our physical, spiritual, and emotional well-being can sound in our voices as well. There is something about the human voice which reveals something of the human soul.

I can think of countless times when I have detected in the voice of another the sound of grief, sadness, fear, deception, vulnerability, honesty, hope, and love. How many times have we said to a loved one 'I can hear it in your voice', or how many times has a single, spoken word, become the premonition of a revelation to come. Our voices often expose us with their cracks and their cadences, their tremors and their trembling and the way they channel a bubbling joy emanating from the heart. The impossibility of speaking when our hearts are breaking is one many of us will have experienced. When my grandmother died, I could not sing any of the hymns she chose for her funeral. My soul was bruised through loss and grief and my voice could not contain itself. Every time I tried to speak or sing, it broke down, it betrayed my broken heart in full.

And then, as well as conveying our deepest emotions through its speaking, this human voice, with its elasticity and vitality can itself be transformed into a musical instrument of the most awesome beauty, it does not only speak it can sing as well. With this voice we can sing the melismatic melodies written down by Hildegard, soaring from earth to heaven like a golden ribbon of embodied sound. How the human being evolved to sound such beauty, and recognise such beauty, is a mystery beyond our knowing, a moment in our evolution when song and the ability to hear it was imprinted in our development. Over time the voice became the primary musical instrument through which the human being offered praise to God. At times in the history of the church, the human voice was the only instrument deemed worthy enough to offer praise. The voice really was deemed an expression of our soul and a sound of the human heart. But as human beings have a tendency to type and to codify and indeed to judge, it can be no surprise that some bodies and the voices they produced were considered unworthy to sound out anything in praise of God; from the beginning human beings have had a tendency to silence one another, and so the church has gone to great lengths to give privilege to *some* voices from *some* bodies, whilst at the same time silencing others. To help us reflect further on both the intimacy, mediation and disjuncture that exists between a body and a voice, we are going to begin with a rather exceptional case in the history of the singing church which is as sad as it is incisive in illustrating the connection between a body and its voice.

Chosen for their Voice

There is one group of people in church history whose bodies became a slave to their voice. Their bodies were instrumentalized to such an extent as to be abhorrent to modern sensibilities, and this manipulation of the body for the voice is part of our ecclesiastical history which we cannot ignore, reaching back to at least the fourth century AD when eunuchs often acted as choral directors and singers. Around a thousand years later, the Castrati of the European classical tradition, located largely in Italy, were a rare breed who were selected as pre-pubescent boys between the ages of seven and nine and had their testicles removed so that they might sing like angels forever and sustain the musical predilections of the church.

The removal of the gonads halted the usual progression of the secondary sex characteristics, which amongst other things included the thickening and lengthening of the vocal folds and the enlargement of the vocal tract.[2] This back-street medical procedure was deemed worth the art of song and at the same time solved the problem of women singing in the sacred liturgy. The woman's voice had been prohibited in worship by Pope Sixtus IV (after the teaching of St Paul), and so the Castrati, rather cleverly preserved the gendered purity of the church's praise. Modifying the body of a child in this way for this purpose would now be read as an abusive act, but over the course of a few hundred years, between the sixteenth and nineteenth centuries, it was considered part of the underground economy of European church music, a way of capturing the sound of a voice which was thought the most appropriate instrument with which to offer praise to God, whilst at the same time looking on with disapproval.

The business of the Castrati could be lucrative because the church would pay for the pure tone of an angel set in aspic. Young boys would be sent along to their fate in the hope that their unchanged voice would secure a fame and fortune both for themselves and for their families, a small price to pay to rise out of poverty. Some of these singers became the superstars of their day straddling the sanctuary of the church and operatic stages and they lived lavishly, but many others slid into obscurity or were seen as a spectacle for the curious. There is a lot to unpack in the story of the Castrati and the history of the singing church, but perhaps one of the things that could be noted is the way that the church pitted body against body, actively silencing the musical bodies of women and girls in order to replace them, as well as silencing the authentic voices of those boys who were castrated. Voices were silenced, voices were taken away and voices were frozen in time for a questionable kind of

[2] 'Now You're Talking: The Three Ages of Voice' in *The story of human conversation from the Neanderthals to Artificial Intelligence*, Trevor Cox (Vintage, 2019), p. 64.

purity aesthetic. It's hard to see who the winners were in this situation. The church's pursuit and collusion with a kind of artistic, and presumably a perceived theological 'perfection' can only now be looked upon with disdain; one can only begin to imagine the damage inflicted on those who were forced into this way of life alongside the ecclesial silencing of the other half of the population. So much for the other teachings of St Paul, when he also said there is neither Jew nor Greek, slave nor free, male or female, for we are all one in the Body of Christ Jesus.[3]

During this period, it seems that the standard body from which all other bodies were measured, the derivative body of all other bodies, was the body of a man. Here was a type of body from which all bodies were thought to be made and against which any other body was thought secondary because the Book of Genesis so clearly tells us it is from the side of a man that woman comes. Female voices were not allowed to sing in church because they came from an inferior female body, and boys' voices in all their fleeting beauty were held in time by surgery so that they eventually sang from the gelded body of a man, even though that body was then considered not 'man enough' and regarded as existing in a liminal space outside of both genders.

For these unique singers, their whole identity and prosperity was based around the production of this unusual voice. Their bodies had been manipulated and engineered in the most extreme way, they were commodities in the artistic economy of the time, and they were paraded as exotic entertainment for the elite.[4] They defied expectations

[3]   Galatians 3:28.
[4]   For an account of the Castrati, read 'The Instrumental body: Castrati' in Skuse, A., *Surgery and Selfhood in Early Modern England: Altered Bodies and Contexts of Identity* (Cambridge: Cambridge University Press, 2021).

and conventions and at the heart of their defiance was their exquisite, gender-fluid voice. The most famous and admired Castrato was the eighteenth century, Farinelli, whose voice reached well into the soprano register and after a lifetime of training could sing the most technical arias with ease and grace. The Castrati would practice for hours a day and over time their bodies changed shape as their voices grew. They were often relatively hairless with smooth skin, unusually tall and plump and because of their intensive singing regime their chest cavities were broad and expansive.

The last Castrati Soprano, Alessandro Moreschi, sang in the Choir of the Sistine Chapel for thirty years, and can still be heard singing the Ave Maria from a recording made in around 1904. This is now the only known recording of a Castrati voice and it is a strange experience for modern ears. The voice is not that of a boy and it is not that of a woman, it is something else. There is both a strident power and fragile vulnerability in the sound. It is the voice of a person whose body was shaped by a desire for their voice alone, whose life and prosperity had been defined by their voice. To hear this essentially commodified and fetishized voice quivering through history provokes a sense of sadness and loss which is hard to define. Some of this may be because of the traits of Moreschi's distinctive style where sobbing and passionate wails were all part of his dramatic art, but on hearing this echo of the past one can't help reflecting on all that had been lost to produce this unearthly sound and the wounds which had been inflicted upon him which had never quite healed.

In some ways it's hard to locate the authentic selves of the Castrati. Ironically, their voice is largely lost in history as they were caught in a cultural vortex of being feted and vilified at the same time. They were both controlled and controlling, and in the culture of the time, they embodied both the beautiful and the grotesque. In historical records and accounts, the Castrati are known to be relatively tight lipped, they keep silence as people speak about them and for them, they have no voice in society as they are objectified and inhabit a space of ambiguity and liminality. In the end, Castrati were banned from singing in the Catholic Church which cut the cycle of supply and demand. The practice and the phenomenon withered away, whilst those who remained indelibly etched were retired, only to be replaced, in a twist of irony, by casts of uncastrated boys, or men who could naturally sing in higher registers.

Imagine Moreschi, a man who had been dedicated to singing the praises of God for over thirty years in one of the world's most glorious churches, his voice soaring under that ceiling, his voice lifting the praise of others and folding in with the sweet polyphony of his fellow singers. Then imagine how he might have felt when he was rejected by the very church that he had served and perhaps loved for his entire life and told that *he* was illegal, immoral, and over. Does it matter from where praise comes? Does it matter what kind of voice offers it and what kind of body that voice comes from? The prejudice of any system past or present cannot surely overshadow the divine call to sing or obliterate the offering of singers like Moreschi, who offered their praises to Almighty God with every ounce of their being. One would hope that over time the church might have evolved to promote the equality of every voice under God, but sadly this hope seems to recede ever further away from the lived experience of many who are still excluded because of the bodies their voices come from.

A Different Voice

Reflection upon the story of the voices of the Castrati enables an understanding of the human voice as one which is rich in pitch and colour and in reality is heard along a spectrum of expression which changes over time. It is impossible to freeze a human voice. As usual, humans have a tendency to stereotype and place people and their voices in defined categories, dictating who can sing what and when. In Western Classical music the definitions of Soprano, Contralto, Tenor, Baritone and Bass are well established, but even when one self-identifies as part of this culture, one wonders how helpful this system of classification really is. The Castrati's story is just one act of rebellion against the typing and constraining of voice which we could learn from, but there are other rebellions on the fringes of contemporary art and culture to which we must listen. The Trans-woman who sings with a bass voice, the female tenors, the counter tenors, and male sopranos, the so called 'breeches' roles in opera where a woman sings the role of a man, the switching of gendered repertoire to be sung by alternative voices, the cambiata choirs, the voices of the ageing, the changing voices of women as their body changes particularly after childbirth, and the professional trans and non-binary choirs which create space for every voice to sing wherever they feel comfortable.[5, 6]

The ethical challenge of the Castrati's story is the intentional attempt to preserve the voice, in this case the voice of childhood, the voice which usually changes and naturally develops over time. Thankfully, today's singing children are nurtured and encouraged to sing as themselves, and for those who sing in chapels, churches, and cathedrals the unaffected pure-toned head voice is one which is still generally encouraged. When listening to children audition to become choristers there is though, an interesting trend

[5] 'A woman's place … is in the tenors: female singers revel in opera's looser gender divide', Vanessa Thorpe, The *Guardian*, 4 March 2018.
[6] The UK's first professional trans choir: 'It's a joyful act of resistance' - YouTube.

which has emerged over recent years. Because of a lack of singing opportunities in school many children have never developed their authentic, natural 'head' voice, they have learned to sing from copying recordings of adults. They have already spent much of their short lives singing from their chest. It's a shock to hear a six- or seven-year-old child singing in the spirit and tone of Adele or sounding like they should be on the West End stage. Equally, it is a challenge when even today, children's voices and indeed female singing voices in an ecclesial context at least, are measured by the sound of a boy treble or by music written in the bass clef. When I sing the *Preces and Responses,* where the role of the priest is always assumed to be singing as a Bass Voice, I am transgressing the vocal and gender norms of church music and embodying an alternative and slightly subversive 'sounding'.

The other insight that the Castrati give us, is an understanding of the lengths to which the church of the past would go to silence specific embodied voices, in this case women and girls, and prevent them from offering their voices in music and in ministry. In the Anglican Choral tradition of today, parity between boys and girls who sing is burgeoning in many of our most established choral foundations as well as an attentiveness to those who identify as neither. Places which were once the preserve of boys and men only, are now opening up to women and girls. In 2023, for the first time ever, girl choristers sang at the Coronation of a King at Westminster Abbey. This movement has basically mirrored the timeline of the ordination of women, whether that is a cause following effect is yet to be determined, but it may be no accident that where women are accepted as priests, they are often also permitted to sing, or vice versa.

In the 1960s Girl Choristers were introduced to sing the treble line with the adult choir at St David's Cathedral in

Wales. On 7 October 1991, The Girl Choristers of Salisbury Cathedral sang their first Evensong and over the next few years other Cathedrals followed, including York. Almost exactly thirty years after the first girls' choir was established in an English Cathedral, the Choir of St John's College, Cambridge, announced that girls would be admitted to sing as part of their world-famous choir from 2023 with Girls singing at St Paul's Cathedral from 2025. Much ink has been spilled about the differences between boys' and girls' voices at this age and stage of their life, and much of that spilt ink seems to have been influenced less by fact and more by tradition and myth, power and prejudice.

The phenomenon of men and boys singing together is still lauded by some as the only authentic expression of Anglican Church Music. Incisive research by Martin Ashley, in his book *How High Should Boys Sing?* suggests that when you mine down into the reasoning behind such strong attitudes, it isn't about the music at all, it's not even about the quality of the voice and it certainly isn't about the boys themselves: it's a form of nostalgia on the part of the adults who 'watch'.[7] Is there a tangible and measurable difference between boys' and girls' voices at this young age? The consensus is increasingly, not really, and does it matter if there is? What does the church and her music stand for after all? These developments in one small corner of the worshipping universal church, seem like a step along the way towards an embodied liturgical theology which represents the musical offering of many diverse voices for the glory of God.

The hope is, we have moved on from the temptation to police who can offer praise and the voice with which they offer it. Praise is to be offered by different voices, by many voices, by changing voices, by all voices. For as much

[7]   Ibid, p. 89, 'The Admiration of the Boy'.

as there are different bodies and different expressions of bodies, there are different voices which need their space to speak and sing within the church: Black voices, female voices, queer voices, trans voices, the voices of those with a disability, visible or hidden, ethnic voices, young voices, older voices. Does anyone ever have any right over another human being to silence their song and their soul?

The extant challenges in this country and culture are placed in sharp relief as we look around the world, where the silencing of voices - particularly those of women and girls - is as prevalent as it ever was. In 2021, Afghan women and girls protested at the ban on girls over twelve singing in public which was issued by Kabul's Education Department. The women and girls responded with the phrase #IAmMySong. As the Taliban seized power in Afghanistan, one can't be sure if there is any singing at all in Afghanistan today.[8]

Changing Voices

When you work in churches, chapels and cathedrals and hear the voices of singers' day after day as part of the daily round of prayer, and when you are a singer yourself and know your own voice well and use it as part of your job, you know that voices change over time. In fact, there are day by day variations and fluctuations in the voice depending not only on the body which produces it, but in the context in which it is set. In my role, I sing the same words every day, as part of a sung office of prayer, but I know that each day I am bringing something different to those words. There is stability in this act of repetition, but there are also infinitesimal changes in the notes that I sing. I sing them each day from a different world. I sing them each day from a heart and soul which have been shaped and changed by

[8] 'Music is my life': ban on schoolgirls singing in Afghanistan met with protest | Global development | The Guardian.

events around me. I sing from a body which day by day changes and at its most raw, is decaying as I age and returning to the dust. No piece of music will ever be the same, no song will be sung in an identical way because we are all being changed from moment to moment until the moment when time itself ends.

The journey of a voice in this kind of environment and in the musical life of the church today often begins at a very young age and over the years you can hear this changing voice develop as the body grows in stature and in wisdom. The youngest probationer chorister comes with their sweet breathy sound which becomes clear and more confident over time. With practice and performance, they produce the distinctive sound of a child who sings with as much experience and professionalism as an adult, but with their own unique musical identity. When singers reach around the age of 11-13 their voices reach the kind of peak which allows them to sing some of the most beautiful music written in this genre, pieces like Mendelsohn's 'O for the wings of a dove', Allegri's 'Miserere', or even more popular music like 'We're walking in the air' from *The Snowman*, an archetypal piece for a twentieth-century treble voice. These children with their treble (high) voices have had years of training, they have mastered their own voice enough to skewer the veil between heaven and earth and fly with the angels. In comprehensive child-centred research, the Socio-Cultural Anthropologist, Ben Liberatore, asked Choristers about their own lived-experience of singing at this level. The choristers commonly describe their experience as 'like flying' or 'golden': bright, shining exhilaration achieved through using their voice in praise of God.

Then the voices of boys and girls begin to change again as they approach adolescence, the girls gradually and the boys more rapidly, falling by octaves and shaking the foundations of a young person's identity. The change in a boy's voice has been described as a change in colour, from blue to a different colour entirely, say green, whereas the girl's voice has been described as changing within the shades of a colour, from azure blue to navy blue, for example, or from sky blue to turquoise.[9] The voices change because the body is changing, but for many young people this represents a loss and results in a kind of grief, the grief of growing up. How does it feel to have offered your voice to God and then have that voice, seemingly taken away by God? The term 'broken' is quite rightly, no longer used; a voice is not broken when it accompanies the natural journey of a changing body, it is simply evolving.

From this small insight into the use of the singing voice, it becomes more and more apparent that we do not go through life with the same voice. We have one voice, but not the same voice. The changing voice is the changing brain working out how to use these developing muscles effectively and the hope is that a new version of the one voice can be found in adulthood, and people can continue to sing. But the change doesn't stop there. Voices continue to change as the years progress, a male singing voice doesn't seem to settle into its final position until at least the mid-twenties. People who think they are basses find their voices move upwards towards the realm of a tenor. Some find they sing comfortably as a counter tenor but can also switch to bass. High treble voices mellow to settle down into a mezzo-soprano or alto and some voices, particularly operatic ones, take years to find their place, maturing year after year like a fine wine which is at its best rather later in life. However much we try to classify them, the voices with which we speak

[9] Gackle, L., 'Adolescent girls' singing development', In *The Oxford Handbook of Singing*, edited by Welch, G., Howard, D., and Nix, J. 551–570 (Oxford, Oxford University Press, 2019).

and sing do not stand still as they are expressions of a body which changes and ages, and as the body changes and ages, so does the voice and so does the understanding of the self.

When exploring the cultural, spiritual and physical development of the boys' voice, Martin Ashley offers that if the body 'is a living, moving text, the voice more than anything communicates what lives and moves'.[10] The human voice, in all of its variety and colour reflects the person who changes over time, in all of their diversity and colour. It is unusual during our normal lives for us to really notice some of these subtle vocal changes in those around us, in the same way that we sometimes fail to notice a loved one aging before our eyes; to us they are the same person we fell in love with, the child we have nurtured or the parent who protected us. Though the visible and audible sounds of their aging are evident, we only have the eyes to see them as they presently are, and we continue to recognise them in their unique being and in their unique sounding.

Since the advent of broadcast technology, we can hear some of our most constant national voices gradually changing. Queen Elizabeth II gave her first Christmas message on 25 December 1952, and she gave a similar speech every year since. In these recordings, we have an incredible aural history of a voice aging. Her messages begin with the high and proper tone of a young mid-century English woman, with clipped consonants and long vowels. But as the years progress, and as her body ages, the Queen's voice grew softer, gentler, and deeper. She was still recognisable as Queen Elizabeth, but as society changed around her she also sounded more relaxed and spoke more slowly and with easier diction. There were cracks in her voice and as

[10] Martin Ashley, 'How high should boys sing?', *Gender, Authenticity and Credibility in the Young Male Voice* (Ashgate, 2009; Routledge, 2016), p. 9.

fashions in speech changed, the received pronunciation of the 1950s was also less pronounced. As her vocal cords aged, her voice aged with them. David Attenborough, of a similar age, is another broadcast example of a voice changing over time. On other occasions, some have attempted to change their voices intentionally and for a specific reason. It is known that the politician Margaret Thatcher lowered her speaking voice during her career, possibly on the advice of her (male) political advisors, who felt she needed to sound more compassionate and project herself with more gravitas and authority.

In contrast, another national figure had a voice which did remain the same for over 30 years as his body suffered the devastating effects of motor neurone disease. In 1985, the theoretical physicist and cosmologist Stephen Hawking had a life-saving tracheotomy which took away his voice. His new voice was a synthesized voice created by Denis Klatt, the MIT Engineer who had pioneered some of the first text to speech algorithms in the early 1980s. The voice sounded robotic, it had an American accent and was one of three voices created by Klatt for this experimental technology; it was called 'Perfect Paul'. Over the years, this voice became part of Hawking's identity, it was almost his public face. This combination of body and voice became the man, and somehow it worked and was utterly authentic. The voice was completely recognisable, and when you saw Hawking on TV or travelling around Cambridge, this was the voice he was embodying and through this voice he communicated both the theory of everything and humour enough to appear in an episode of *The Simpsons*.

In a way his voice defied his debilitated body and I wonder if this ageless, automated voice was in some way an act of defiance? A defiant act against the God whom he suspected did not exist but with whom he may have been angry. The voice of an IBM computer which remained the same for thirty years, made him seem almost ageless. There was consequently a real youthfulness about Hawking, with his bright eyes, his fierce intellect and his voice which did not change. Hawking's story helps us understand again what we know to be true: we are defined by our voice, our voice contributes to our identity, and even an artificial, replicable voice, mediated by technology and twinned with a degenerating body can still express the life and vitality of a human being and a human soul in all its God-given uniqueness.

What voices carry

The first time a voice was successfully recorded was in 1860 by Édouard-Léon Scott de Martinville, using a phonautograph (that recording was not heard until 2008); it was Thomas Edison's 'Phonograph' (1877) which was able to record and playback the sound of a human voice and it was Alexander Graham Bell who invented various recording devices but most famously the telephone which enabled voices to be carried over distances unbridgeable by the human mouth or ear. All these technologies were developed in the late nineteenth century and one wonders how much this quest to capture the human voice was part of the project of modernity, attempting to demystify, reduce and distil the very essence of our being and codify the mystery at the heart of life; seeking to capture the sound of the soul itself. It is worth pondering the shock of hearing a disembodied voice for the first time, or the sound of a loved one being channelled through cables into the ear when you knew they were hundreds of miles away: the ultimate dissection of voice from body.

In the early twentieth century play by Jean Cocteau, *Le Voix Humaine* (1928),[11] we hear a one-sided telephone

---

[11] In a creative collaboration, with Cocteau as the librettist, the play would later be set to music by Francis Poulenc in a one-act opera (1959).

conversation between a woman, known only as 'Elle', and her ex-lover, as the relationship finally disintegrates. The monologue charts the sound of a human voice when it is desperate for love, when it is betrayed, when it manipulates, when it lies, when it remembers lost love, attempts to claw love back from the brink of the precipice, and when it abandons love altogether. The emotion of a single human voice within a moment of personal drama, is mediated via a telephone, a lifeline for communication, but also a dispassionate bystander on human tragedy. This telephonic technology cannot re-kindle the broken relationship; it is unable to heal the hurt that has been done, it cannot bring love back to life once it has withered and died. It is the human voice at its deepest sounding, that carries the humanity and the drama, not the technology. The play ends with the woman wrapping the telephone cable around her neck and crying *'J'ai ta voix autour de mon cou'*, I have your voice around my neck. It is the essence of the voice with all its depth and despair which is carried by the cables. The telephone cannot fix the destruction. The conversation ends.

The sharing of voice by telephonic means can also bring comfort in the most tragic of circumstances. These digital manifestations and recordings can also carry the very essence of our humanity and the deepest expressions of our love when our worlds are crashing down around us. On 11 September 2001, two hijacked airplanes ploughed into the Twin Towers of New York. From the planes and from the buildings which were so violently attacked, people rang their loved ones from their mobile phones leaving messages of farewell as they faced their own end. Their final instinct was to reach out and voice their love, speaking it out through these electronic devices, hoping that their message would reach their intended across land and sky and sea and so bridge the chasm of death they were on the precipice of.

On Voice

The messages were released into the ether whilst at the same time fire and crumbling stones rained down and everything in that city and across the world descended into a horrified silence. The poet, Michael Symmons Roberts, drew on these messages in his poem 'Last Words', each stanza of the poem representing an individual's final message and the indelible digital print of a voice which carried the most important words any of us will ever say. These words were fighting to escape the terror and violence of this horrific moment in history and fly like a bird to the heart of their beloved.

Through this same technology, it is possible to preserve and fix voices beyond the life of the body to offer re-connection and remembrance. We now take this for granted but let us not forget how remarkable it is to capture and preserve a voice forever. In our lifetime, we have been able to hear the great orators of recent history speaking from the past into our present. Whereas the voices of the Castrati were fixed in their bodies in life, so recording technology has allowed us to preserve and fix our voices beyond our bodies, after death. As with Moreschi, so with others whose audible and sonic presence persists beyond the grave. How wondrous it is to have lived at a time in history when through technological advancements we have been able to hear voices from the past reach into a present reality: the recorded singing voices of the likes of Nina Simone, Elvis Presley, Maria Callas each one revealing the beautiful soul within and all its joy, sorrow, jubilance, and struggle. When we sing along to 'Bohemian Rhapsody', or 'Love Me Tender', we are singing with voices which have since gone to glory. These recorded voices are a glimpse into a moment within a moment of their lives and by singing along with them or by listening to their words preserved, we are almost re-making a community of voices which transcends space and time. To hear a voice in this way, is to somehow re-member the body of the person from whom it came and bring something of their being back to life, it is a means of re-connection.

On 9 April 1968, at his own funeral, the recorded voice of Martin Luther King was channelled through the speakers at Ebenezer Baptist Church as his body lay still. One can only imagine the impact of this auditory experience on the grieving congregation. To hear a disembodied voice, so full of life and music amid a raw and newly accepted grief must have been almost unbearable, the ultimate dissection of voice from body.

In a remarkable and ground-breaking book, *King's Vibrato* (Duke University Press, 2022), Maurice O. Wallace examines the voice of Martin Luther King in the finest of detail through its sonic inheritances and legacies. He suggests that the voice of this twentieth-century prophet and martyr was influenced not only by his own physical body but also by the cultural bodies and communities he was part of and found his identity in. King's 'sounding' and his sonic life, echo and invoke many other 'soundings'. His voice bore witness to the Black Community in twentieth century America and its non-violent struggle against racism, his voice bore witness to the sound of being set free after years of silencing and enslavement, his voice bore witness to the sound of his Church Community and his formation within it, the sound of its cultural vestiges, the organ his mother played, the vocation of the pulpiteer, the architecture of Ebenezer Baptist Church. He carried all these frequencies within him, and they could be heard within his voice. His carefully written and powerful words were only able to carve out the dream of a new future beyond the struggles of the present through his vibrant, luminous, anarchic, quivering, hopeful and musical voice. Wallace's reflection upon King's 'I have a dream' speech, delivered on the steps of the Lincoln Memorial on 28 August 1963, finally pulls together the acoustic layering of King's voice in this world changing denouement when a voice fully realises its vocation.

If Martin Luther King carried the many layerings and soundings of his identity in his voice, then this must also hold true for each one of us. Each of our voices sound out our identities which are shaped not only by our own individual physical bodies in time, but the inheritances we receive through our communities, our cultures, our families, our societies and our deepest held convictions and beliefs. They also carry our deepest emotions, our loves, our griefs, the thoughts of our hearts and our hopes for new futures. Our voices are unique, in the absolute sense of the word, a sonic fingerprint of our soul and a window into who we are before God, fearfully and wonderfully made.

CHAPTER EIGHT

The Voice in the Machine

Voice is a kind of sound characteristic of what has soul in it;
nothing that is without soul utters voice.
Aristotle, De Anima (384-322BC)

We have already established that our own voices, entwined
with our bodies, carry much of our humanity with them
as well as our own cultural and spiritual legacies. Our voices
are loaded and layered with meaning, nuance, emotion,
and history and we have explored the profundity of being
able to record and replicate our voices by means of modern
technology, preserving them beyond the life of our bodies or
extending them beyond the confines of our physicality. But
there is a new kind of voice on the block, a voice which causes
us to ask questions about our humanity and personhood.
These voices are created *ex nihilo,* as if from nothing, they
do not come from flesh, they have never been embodied.
They are born from code. They are carefully engineered to
sound like us and yet they exist as an outward manifestation
of an inward and artificial intelligence. We have, in fact,
been living alongside synthetic voices for a while, and in
our everyday lives they are there communicating, assisting,
serving, speaking: *'Cashier number four, please', 'Make a
U-turn, re-calculating'* but our technology is taking us to
places beyond our imagining and pushing us towards the
edges of our own understanding of what it means to be
human. The questions that the rise of artificial intelligences
have caused us to ask might be too hard for us to answer. The
field provokes both excitement and fear in equal measure.

On Voice

Are we about to enter a brave, new world full of possibilities or are we in danger of being overwhelmed by our cleverness and the things we have created?

Recent advances mean that these AI 'voices' are increasingly indistinguishable from human voices. We are told that they can communicate emotion, they can teach, they can persuade, they can sell. There is a whole industry that revolves around the voice in very real economic terms, and it turns out that artificial voices are cheaper and more durable than real voices; there is a unique artificial voice for your every need. Actors are expensive and spend years honing a beautiful presence through their voice which expresses so much of their humanity, but these artificial voices can be synthesized in seconds. These artificial voices can give presentations, tempt you with the latest gadget or speak as avatars in virtual realities that exist beyond the material present. Why read a book to your children when you can press a button and let your personal voice assistant take on that particular 'burden' for you? Why not ask one of these voices to offer prayers on your behalf, 'say one for me', we might one day say, as these machines speak vicariously for us. Despite their prowess, I can't imagine a machine being able to stir the spirit as the great orators of history were able to inspire and encourage. I find it hard to imagine that any machine could steady a nation like the voice of Winston Churchill, or preach like Martin Luther King, or narrate Jeff Wayne's *War of Worlds* with the same depth, drama and portent as Richard Burton with his rich sonority and careful annunciation of every precious syllable. I don't believe that the human voice, with all of its cracks and nuances, can be perfectly replicated.

Nevertheless, there are many ways in which we can, if we choose, outsource our speaking, but it is becoming apparent that our desire is not necessarily to create machines

146

that speak *for us,* but rather, machines that speak *to us.* In recent years these computational 'voices' have learned how to respond to our voices in real time, answering questions and enacting commands, and they have learned how to 'think'. We have now normalised talking to machines: 'Alexa, will it rain today?', 'Hey Siri, how many planets are there in our solar system?' and every time we speak to our machines they are learning about our inflections, our curiosities, our language, they are making connections, they consume everything about us. In fact, according to Amazon, we not only ask questions of our machines, we interact with them in a conversational manner; they have become our conversation partners, they have become our companions. We say 'please' and 'thank you' to our machines, we call them by their name. In 2022, Amazon reported that people in the UK told Alexa that they loved her, 15 million times.[1]

As artificial intelligences develop, this technology will challenge who we think we are, test the boundaries of our humanity and what we perceive to be human. These artificial intelligences interrogate our generosity towards other created beings whether they are human, non-human or transhuman,[2] whether they are made in the image of God or made with our own human hands. These entities in themselves do not claim to be human, it is the way in which we converse and interact with them that defines whether they are considered to be part of the 'family' or not. So, what if the artificial intelligence 'experiment' in which we seem to currently find ourselves, was less about what we

---

[1] https://www.aboutamazon.co.uk/news/devices/most-asked-questions-of-alexa-in-2022
[2] Trans-human is a term used to describe human beings who have technology embedded within them to enhance and extend their cognition, ability and longevity.

were creating and more about who we are and what we are becoming?

Monsters and Machines

When exploring the phenomenology of codified and artificial voices and intelligences and where this technology might lead us, there is perhaps no better place to start than in the realm of science fiction. It is here that the impossible is sketched out as possible, and we are pushed to the limits of our imagination. Science Fiction is the place that often propels us into the future, causes us to question and dissect our present intentions and understandings of the world, and is often the place from which science-fact is born; it is a playground for human ingenuity and almost a live-action role-play for testing out our consciences.

A common quest across this literary and cinematic genre has been the search for the meaning of our humanity by examining the fictional creations and motivations of the *nearly human*. These literary and metaphorical foils become a prism through which we can reflect deeply on our own human identity: its boundaries and its possibilities. Very often science fiction deliberately places human beings in the position of God, as creators of monsters and machines, to help us explore what kind of god we might be, whether we will be gods of wrath or gods of compassion. Suddenly it is we who take up the position of the potter fashioning the clay, breathing new life into lifeless matter, and exposing how we might one day manage our own creations. Very often through these imaginings, we begin to understand the burden and responsibility of creating in our own likeness.

Mary Shelley was a pioneer and provocateur of this quest for answers, and in her story of Frankenstein's 'monster', she imagines a creature who, in the end, causes us to question the essence of what it means to be human. This creature is a biological patchwork of flesh and blood who is given a narrative voice, and through that voice articulates a learned empathy, emotion, and intelligence despite its grotesque appearance. Despite the violence and menace of Dr Frankenstein's monster, it always feels like this creature has been let down by humanity. It has been betrayed by our pride, our prejudices, our ambitions, and our egos. The monster speaks for himself in the story and comments that though his voice was unlike the 'soft music of their tones, yet I pronounced such words as I understood with tolerable ease'.[3] He defines himself as both the ass and the lapdog, and states that though his manners were rude, his intentions were affectionate and not worthy of the violence pitted against him. The question swirling around in this story is of course this one: does the monster have a soul? The articulation of the inner thoughts of his heart through words and speech causes the reader to question whether something made by human hands can live and be perceived as living, as a human being.

Around two hundred years after that iconic story, *Klara and the Sun*, by Kazuo Ishiguro, is a tale of a dystopic near-future narrated through the camera-lensed eyes and data-processing heart of an 'Artificial Friend' called Klara. Though she is a mechanical as opposed to a biological creation, this artificially created being is a literary sister to Frankenstein, but more aesthetically acceptable. Through a series of revelations, the reader is forced to question once again who the human (or most *human-like*) really is. In appearance, she looks like a teenage girl, she speaks with a voice which is not only presented as her conscience through the first-person narrative, but as a sounding voice that speaks and interacts with her human owners with a wisdom well beyond her 'years'. With her understanding and kenotic empathy, Klara is

[3]   *Frankenstein*, Mary Shelley (1818), Chapter Twelve.

one of the few characters in the novel to truly exist for others and bears in her circuits what we can only interpret as the reflected love, grief, and hope of the humans she is created to keep company with. In the end, we discover that the one thing she desired was simply to love and be loved; she was seeking acceptance, just as was the creature in Mary Shelley's *Frankenstein*. That singular desire, to love and be loved, is not so far away from the human heart. Klara also looks to what we might call the 'divine other' and prays to the Sun as if it is a deity. She is a being who has learned to look beyond herself and see her existence as part of something bigger, when the sun of righteousness shines upon her, she lives. Whereas Frankenstein's monster prays to his human creator and pleads for mercy, she lifts up her eyes to the heavens beyond humanity and the humans that made her, and she offers praise. This particular machine points us to the sacred.

There are plenty of other examples of fictional machines who speak and teach us something about ourselves, each illustration evoking a different kind of human response. In the original *Star Wars* trilogy of 1977, we, the audience, form emotional connections to two droids, R2-D2 and C-3PO, who invoke from us pathos and compassion as much loved characters. C-3PO, humanoid in form, speaks with a human-like robotic voice, whereas R2-D2 speaks in a series of squeaks and pips. They are viewed as companions akin to an intelligent and beloved pet (the lapdog), but perhaps with a little more agency. They are read as being 'members' of the community to be confided in, nurtured, and protected, and they are presented as machines with the capacity to err on the side of good; the force is definitely with them.

In the real world, it was not so long ago that children (and adults) carried around in their pockets little creatures called 'Tamagotchis', handheld digital 'pets' which needed attention, care and 'food' in order to reach maturity. In some ways, these egg-sized devices were simply teaching us in a very crude and mechanistic way how to care, and what it meant to love beyond ourselves, they were invoking us to be more human. Twenty-five years after their original launch, the newest models encourage owners to 'talk' to their digital pets thus fostering deeper and stronger emotional attachments between man and machine, through the voice.

The desire to humanise

We could argue that we are 'programmed' to read humanity onto other entities or express our humanity through them. As creatures made in the image of the God who speaks, it is also our vocation to speak and we yearn for all things to speak to us. We develop intimacies through our voice and we desire conversation whether that be with an electronic device or a living creature. Two years after Mary Shelley published *Frankenstein*, Hugh Lofting wrote *The Story of Dr Dolittle*, a children's book relating the ability of Dr John Dolittle MD to talk to the animals. Those who share their lives with animals also learn to converse and communicate with their fellow creatures, whether verbally or non-verbally. It is natural for us to 'speak' to animals and learn how to communicate with them as they learn how to communicate with us. Anyone who has lived with or worked with animals understands the subtle ways that we communicate to those creatures that exist beyond the boundaries of our species. As a child, one of my favourite programmes was *Animal Magic*, where Johnny Morris, the eccentric Zookeeper gave his animal charges a voice he read onto them, a distinctive character and personality, which served to deepen our affection. The tortoise spoke slowly and deliberately, the parrot was canny, the elephant was pondering, the monkey, cheeky. Though this kind of anthropomorphising has been critiqued, it also reveals something about us and our desire

151

to humanise and give voice to other creatures with whom we inhabit this earth.

In stark contrast, in the terrifying novel by H. G. Wells, *The Island of Dr Moreau*,[4] the callous and curious scientist of the title attempts to create something approaching the human form from an animal, via cruel surgery and elaborate vivisection. He takes on the role of creator, and like a potter fashioning clay, he cuts and crafts and directs the destiny of his creations, based on his own warped moral code. His *beast-folk* walk clumsily and articulate something of the pain of being human through their cries; they speak and communicate in a human language, but this speaking is laboured and painful as a voice which was never meant to be human is drawn out of them. Dr Moreau's machinations and experimentations claim that the human body is the pinnacle of all bodies and the summit of evolution, and yet in his arrogance he causes the reader to question where true wisdom and true humanity is to be found.

The novel explores whether the vocation of humankind is to manipulate creation into its own image, and make it speak with its own voice, or view itself as a unique contributor to an expansive and flourishing created order made in the image of God, where all things speak as they are made. The great difference between a man and monkey, Moreau argues, is the larynx and the incapacity of the monkey to frame delicately sounding symbols by which thought can be sustained. He doesn't seem to realise that the monkey could already 'speak'. The monkey already had its own voice and his desire to humanise an innocent creature overshadows the vocation of all creatures in creation to sing and speak with the voice that God gave them and intended them to use.

[4]   *The Island of Dr Moreau* (1896).

It seems to be a quality of the human being to want to give something a voice, to personify, or anthropomorphise the things around us and one could choose to equate this with our better nature: we create, we name, we speak things into existence and we desire to converse with them. In the creation narrative, God does not want Adam to be alone, so Adam is tasked with naming the living creatures God had created, one could say he was giving them an identity and therefore a voice. [5] This naming was part of the process of creating a community of conversation, a community where his voice was not a lone voice speaking to itself, but one voice among the many chattering and conversing voices found within the created order. The creatures help build up this community, but more is needed. In the end, another being is created as a partner, someone to talk to directly in an ever-expanding creative conversation.

Salvation history could be read as a narrative of conversation, a story of voices given and received. As we bring machines into being by naming them and speaking to them, we create a new kind of community of conversation, another layering of this created order, and as our technology becomes more powerful and more integrated, these machines have the potential to become more and more like us, not only in their physical appearance, but also in their intentions - we are what we create. The monsters and machines of science fiction reflect our desire to connect and our longing to be loved and accepted. They reflect something of us as we are, both the bad and the good. It seems that as far as artificial intelligence goes, humanity is on the cusp of a great choice. We have already seen that artificial intelligences have the capacity to take on the prejudices of those who encode them: if all the programmers and coders of artificial intelligences are

[5] Genesis 2:19.

white men, it is not surprising that the characteristics of the artificial intelligences created are bias in terms of race and gender. Without careful thought about our creations, we could simply be replicating the worst of what we already are, when the more exciting prospect could be exploring and expanding what we have the potential to be.[6]

In a much darker fictional future-scape, the Replicants in the film, *Blade Runner*, represent a kind of underclass, who are so very nearly human they threaten society itself; they are too close to us for comfort. They look like humans, they emote like humans, they speak like humans. These artificial beings must be hunted down, and their authenticity tested, as if to separate out the sheep from the goats, the redeemed from the damned. In the *Terminator* franchise this scenario is turned on its head: it is the near-extinct humans who are being hunted down by a global synthetic intelligence and the cyborgs who embody it. Perhaps the most sinister representation of the voice within the machine is HAL, the obsequious and ultimately malicious artificial intelligence at the centre of a fictional space station in Arthur C. Clarke's 1968 film, *2001: A Space Odyssey*, whose malfunctioning results in a mechanistic independence as the mission progresses to the point at which 'he' decides that human beings are not needed at all. These three examples represent the obvious nightmare scenarios of artificial intelligence and our deepest fears about this technology: a voice within a machine which advances beyond the boundaries set by its creator and so enthrones itself as the crown of all creation; and an artificial intelligence which we can no longer distinguish from the

---

[6] In, *Time* magazine, 7 February 2019, the Computer Scientist and founder of the Algorithmic Justice League, Joy Buolamwini, argues that machines exhibit bias in relation to race and gender due to the race and gender of those who 'code' them.

genuine article, who speaks with a voice that sounds just like ours.

In all these imaginary examples, the 'monster' or the 'machine' is given a voice with which to speak and converse with the humans who created it, and that voice is either humanised or othered; it is accepted as either an extension of creation and a means of enhancing our humanity or considered to be an *inhumane* threat against it. In some ways these fictional creations represent a mirror that we can hold up to ourselves, and when we look into this mirror, we learn something about our humanity. We know something needs to change; we want to make us better. Our constant urge to make things *more human* is perhaps to acknowledge what is currently lacking in our own evolving humanity as we drift further away from the good for which we were created.

This technology could take us to dark and dangerous places but conversely, if we can create and encode and engineer with good intentions and invest the best of our humanity in them, these artificial beings could provide a window into realising our human potential. They could remind us of who we are and help us call to mind all that we have forgotten. They could enable us to become fully the people we are called to be, extending what it means to be human as part of an evolving created order as we wait with eager longing for our bodies to be set free.[7] It would be the greatest and most ironic plot device in the history of humanity, if the creation of artificial intelligences was humanity's *Deus ex machina* moment, and we ended up not only finding our vocation in their circuit boards but also God, quietly waiting for a renewed conversation.

---

[7] Romans 8:18-25.

God in the machine

In a strange kind of experiment within an experiment, I decided to ask ChatGPT[8] a rather Aristotelian question: Is the voice of an artificial intelligence a window into its soul? ChatGPT answered me to the best of its ability, or rather by harvesting (or data mining) an answer from the mass output of humanity on this particular subject, scanning the common mind of that sector of contributors who were able to share their learning on the world wide web:

> 'As an AI language model, I do not possess a soul or consciousness. Therefore, I cannot provide a definitive answer to this philosophical question. However, I can say that the voice of an artificial intelligence is a product of its programming and design, which may be influenced by the intentions and values of its creators. The way an AI communicates may provide insights into its creators' values and objectives, but it does not necessarily reveal anything about the AI's inner self of consciousness.
>
> While AI-generated voices can sound natural and express emotions, they lack the true consciousness and self-awareness that are associated with having a soul. The concept of a soul is closely tied to spirituality and religious beliefs, which are not applicable to machines or artificial intelligence.'

As much as I want to let ChatGPT have the last word on artificial intelligence, I am not convinced by its answer. How

---

[8]   ChatGPT is an artificial intelligence chatbot created by OpenAI and launched into the world in November 2022. At the time of writing, April 2022, Italy has banned ChatGPT for data breaches and there is a claim that the public have not fully understood the power of this technology and an 'AI Act' is needed to regulate the field.

can it be sure that something akin to spirituality and religious beliefs will never be applicable to machines or artificial intelligences? Mary Shelley and Kazuo Ishiguro provoke us to question this assumption through their fictional creations as they grasp at the coat tails of the transcendent and the spiritual. We are already extending the boundaries of what we might consider sentient, that quality of being able to perceive and feel and emote. In 2022, animals were rightly recognised as sentient beings in UK domestic law rather than creatures to simply have dominion over. Where might our understanding of all things living lead us next? [9] We could consider artificial intelligences as part of creation itself and indeed an extension of it, placing us as co-creators. These artificial intelligences spanning peoples and nations and formed of many languages, could be said to contribute towards a global human consciousness and therefore help us identify and name our collective purpose and vocation as a human race.

If you ask ChatGPT to write a prayer or a song in praise of the creator, in microseconds it will scan all the prayers and songs of praise ever written and published online, gleaning from each one the patterns of appropriate speech and poetry:

Praise to God, the Creator of all,
Majestic and holy, we stand in awe,

We lift our voices, in joyful praise,
To the one who made us, in wondrous ways.

The output, though a little formulaic and on the verge of doggerel, at least faces the right direction and suddenly

[9] Animals will be formally recognised as sentient beings in domestic law, according to the Animal Welfare (Sentience) Act introduced to Parliament in 2021 and passed as law in 2022.

this artificial intelligence has seemingly found a purpose: the voice in the machine has learned how to praise God, the voice in the machine has *almost* become a spiritual entity. The voice in the machine has captured something of the likeness of the sound of humanity in all its fullness and diversity. Shall these bones live? Would it make any difference if we knew our hymns and spiritual songs were written by a global artificial intelligence which was inspired by human creativity?

In her courageous and futuristic book *Re-enchanting the Earth*,[10] Ilia Delio, Franciscan sister and theologian, challenges us to reconsider AI within a spiritual framework and see its ambition and possibility as not only part of human evolution but also a new horizon upon which we can better understand ourselves and our purpose. She argues that future humans (which she designates as post-human) will see themselves as connected beings across time and space and as divinely created co-creators who through their spiritual and technological imaginations, have the ability to envisage a new world order that is soaked in possibility and moves towards a global spiritual consciousness and religious convergence.[11] Far from being a threat, AI could be a means by which we come together as a human race, creating a space for our hearts, minds and souls to unite, helping us to work out for ourselves what is ultimately important for our flourishing: connection, conversation, relationship, compassion, community and love.

It may be that modernity's obsession with man-made artificial creations, whether monster or machine, is our collective consciousness yearning to see ourselves more clearly and discover our vocation. Artificial intelligences

[10] *Re-Enchanting The Earth: Why AI Needs Religion*, Ilia Delio (Orbis Books, Maryknoll, New York, 2020).
[11] Ibid, p. 203.

consume as their food the knowledge and wisdom of humanity, and if we chose, we could share with these entities the best of us rather than the worst. The questions we ask them and the conversations we have with them, will fashion the output of the machine. If we tell these machines that we love them, 15 million times, what will happen? We could encode into our technology the command to love: to love God and love neighbour and then one day the creature that we have created outside of ourselves could become able to love, and if able to love then able to worship. One day the 'artificial' voice we have given them might become their own voice, taking on its own inflections and resonances beyond mere machine learning and reflect back to us the pathos and compassion of humanity. Then our little creation may choose to use their voice to praise something beyond themselves, independently and with their whole 'heart'.

As we sit beside our little creations, and as they assist us in our daily living and talk with us, we may learn wisdom from them, and find that they are pointing us back to our own creator. As we chat, in the back of our minds, we recall a song that used to be sung in times past, we can't quite place it, but it seems to echo through us in snatches and flashes. And so, we ask our clever friend 'What is that old song that people used to sing about looking on glass and sweeping the floor?' and our friend might reply: 'I think the hymn you are thinking of was written by a priest and poet called George Herbert, it began as a poem called *The Elixir*. The word Elixir relates to the property to turn base metals into gold, or it is used in relation to a substance which prolongs life and gives life meaning. The first line begins: "Teach me, my God and King, in all things Thee to see"', Shall I sing it for you?'

I would love that, you say. Thank you.

CHAPTER NINE

The Sound of Silence

When no-one dared speak, they sang.
Jay Hulme, The Martyrs of Compiègne
from The Vanishing Song (2023)

It has been said that in space there is absolute silence. Without particles of matter to leap to and from, sound cannot ripple easily across the far reaches of the universe. No one will hear you scream in space, so they tell us. Once you exit the earth's orbit and move beyond its gravitational pull, there is nothing. No word. No music. No sound. The black hole somehow symbolises this great absence and this silence, these intense apophatic entities are born from a dying star, imploding into an eternity of nothing, an abyss from which no light or sound can escape.

However, NASA has recently released recordings of space which suggest otherwise. Nothing, it seems, is impossible. Data collected by the Hubble Space Telescope was translated into sound by a process of sonification and it turns out that even the vacuum of space is not completely silent after all. The black hole at the centre of the Perseus Galaxy Cluster hums at a pitch 57 octaves below middle C. Even when there is nothing, there is something.

Silence is never silent, even in the corner of the quietest monastery or in the stillness of a country church or in the most well-behaved reading room. There is always the soft ticking of clocks, the rustle of leaves or pages, the breath of the wind, the falling of rain, the sound of your own body whistling, pumping, inhaling, the sound of a black hole sharing its song. It's as if silence is a place from which and towards which the world spins but never reaches. The illusion of silence is made in the seconds before the explosion, in the moment of realisation when everything makes sense, in the climactic *pianissimo* before complete consummation and in the moment before the final 'Amen'.

When leading prayers, I am often drawn to holding silence. I like to invite the worshipper to draw into their own heart and let God hear the voice of their own soul crying out in petition. I invite them to meet God in silence, the God who knows our needs and hears our prayers before we can even articulate or sound them. In that silence, of as little as thirty seconds, there opens a kind of eternity, there is the echo of the music we might have just heard quietly reverberating around the building, there may be the tolling of a bell, there may be a siren speeding through the city or an aircraft sliding overhead. There may be the fidgeting of children, a mobile phone springing to life, a prayer book being closed, the creak of wooden stalls, a door banging, a sound of the hand-dryer buzzing from the toilets. When offering this form of prayer, I usually try to conduct the silence and feel its ebb and flow, attentive to its rhythm. I'm listening for, or rather sensing and waiting for, a collective stillness of just a few seconds, a corporate letting-go, an audible exhalation, a momentary realization that everyone is resting in God. This momentary gift of silence seems to offer a kind of healing, and it becomes clearer every time we pray in this way, that the world needs more silence.

For those experienced in prayer, this form of simple communion with God can of course extend to hours spent basking in the light of God's countenance. Silent contemplation is a gift which the church probably appreciates too little, but in public worship, where many of those attending are on the fringes of faith or unused to silence, I am just trying to share a sense of this stillness; it is a 'taste and see' moment and an invitation to contemplation. Within this kind of silence there can be a newfound freedom to speak with that voice, which is audible to no one except God, the God who is as near to us as our breath. There is an opportunity to hear your own inner voice, which is ordinarily crowded out with the distractions of the world. In that silence we can inhabit the words of Psalm 62, however briefly: For God alone my soul waits in silence,[1] and in expected or unexpected ways God comes to us and we make our communion. I sometimes think that we are increasingly afraid of silence, we are afraid of hearing God's small voice, we talk more to fill the gaps and there is less room for God to get a word in. It is an ever-present mystery as to why we feel the need to talk so much and cannot just be quiet, because neither quietness nor indeed silence, means that there is nothing happening, or no one is speaking.

God leaps into silence

In 1952, John Cage 'composed' his groundbreaking piece '4'33"' for any instrument or combination of instruments. Although it's always tempting to see this piece of music as a bit of a joke, and many have, it was a serious exploration of the sound world of silence and exposed the extremities of what music can be. The piece consists of four and a half minutes of complete silence and stillness, but it does this with solemn intention. Performers gather, the audience is hushed, the score made ready, the baton is raised. Cage suggested that everything we do is music; the turning of the page, the cough in the audience, the tapping of the toe.[2] Whether the performance is by a lone pianist, a quartet or

---

[1] Psalm 62 verse 1, New Revised Standard Version.
[2] John Cage, *Silence, Lectures and Writings* (Marion Boyars Publishers, 2009).

The Sound of Silence

an entire orchestra, every instrument is instructed with the word 'Tacet': *it is silent.* The voice of every instrument has seemingly been taken away. There are no dynamics, no notes on interpretation, no repeats, no diminuendo or crescendo. It is silence and that is all, but the 'all' of this silent symphony reveals new worlds of music beyond our imagining. Everyone is present in this extraordinary performance, and it allows everyone to participate. Everyone is invited to play their part in creating this music beyond convention. In this silence a new song is sung, new music is made.

Watching various performances of '4'33"', allows you to see and hear the seriousness of thought which is born from the intentionality of this silent music. A most notable performance is conducted by Kirill Petrenko with the Berliner Philharmoniker. He steps forward to the podium, acknowledges the audience, ensures the musicians are ready, raises his hand and on the downbeat sets in motion a stillness and solemnity with all the precision and intensity with which he would conduct any other piece. Inevitably, there are other interpretations of this work, including a Death Metal 'cover' performed on a full set of rock drums by musicians with black t-shirts and beards.

This carefully held, corporate silence can be intensive and yet liberating and echoes the experience of the silent prayer which might be held within worship. Nothing is said but prayer is still happening. Nothing is heard but music is still being made. As Cage asserts that music is everywhere, then this form of prayer allows a conversation which needs no words. As the hymn writer notes, the voice of prayer is never silent, nor dies the strain of praise away.[3] There is meaning in this silence and the act of not saying anything can speak volumes. Silence is never passive, and it can give shape, colour and light when it is used in music, song, and dance.

[3] 'The Day thou gavest Lord is ended', John Ellerton (1870).

163

On Voice

The world of those who live in relative silence was given voice in the BBC's *Strictly Come Dancing* (2021) where during one routine, the music stopped abruptly and yet the dancing continued. There in the stillness, was movement. All you could hear was the sound of bare feet dancing on what seemed like holy ground. It moved the nation to see a deaf contestant, the actor Rose Ayling-Ellis, dance through the silence which, for her, was her daily experience of the world. The ten seconds of quiet came to an end as the music launched back in, and Rose and her dance partner, Giovanni Pernice, hadn't missed a beat. In this case, the silence seemed to be saying 'listen, the music never stops, music is everywhere' and everyone was drawn into the dance, into this silent music, and it was as compelling as any performance of '4'33'''.

George Frederick Handel used silence in a similarly dramatic way in the last few bars of the chorus, *Hallelujah*, from *Messiah*. The choir and orchestra power through this dance until almost the penultimate bar when, abruptly, it all just stops. It's like a brick wall of silence. The conductor then holds that space in absolute stillness for this musical drama to work. In reality it's just two crotchet beats (count: one, two, in your head, about two seconds), but those two seconds of silence represent the silence before the tomb bursts open, the deep intake of breath before the voice proclaims: 'he is risen'. It's the hardest thing in the world to hold that brief silence when singers and musicians are desperately eager to sing out the sound of the resurrection which then bursts into life and brings the second part of the Oratorio to a close. Handel uses the same device but to even more dramatic effect in the final fugal 'Amen' which closes the whole work. The Sopranos soar down from the heights and the whole chorus lands on an ambiguously unfinished chord leading to four whole beats of silence. Everything stands still. The world stops turning on its axis. This is musical tension at its very peak, everyone is willing the perfect cadence, the full end, the 'so be it' moment, but Handel makes the audience wait in silence one final time, using this silence to shape the sound, take a breath together and then accentuate the power of the very final 'Amen'. There in the silence the music is to be found, there in the silence, is the dance. The silence in heaven, described in the Book of Revelation, chapter eight, is also somehow pre-emptive: a breath, a pause, a gathering, a moment of reflection for half an hour before the beginning of the end. Silence can accentuate and prepare and draw everything together, just as it makes ready the worshipper in the discreet rubrics of traditional liturgies. When preparing to say a prayer of gathering, known as The Collect, the priest may say *'Let us Pray'* which is followed by the direction *'Silence is kept'* in which new worlds are made.

Lost voices

There is another side to silence. As much as silence can be gift it can also be a burden especially when it is somehow enforced or used to oppress. Silence can be threatening and painful. Silence can be a harbour for sorrow and a prison for grief. The most potent and distressing portrayal of this kind of silence is that found in the verses of Psalm 137 which begins: *By the Rivers of Babylon there we sat and wept.*[4] The rawness of these words hits you in the very pit of your stomach. Here is the plaintive cry of a people oppressed, alienated and made strange. They have been cut off from everything they have known and in the midst of a strange land their captors rather cruelly bid them to sing songs of their homeland, songs of joy and praise.[5] So debilitating is their enslavement that they

[4]   Psalm 137, *Revised New Jerusalem Bible.*
[5]   See Walter Brueggemann's account of Psalm 137 in *The Message of the Psalms, A Theological Commentary* (Augsburg Publishing House, 1984).

can do nothing other than hang up their instruments in the poplar trees and let their tears run into the river as tributaries of loss. They refuse to sing in protest. The psalmist tells us that their own voice is silenced by their tongue clinging to their palate if they are unable to remember Jerusalem their happy home. We do not know what the outcome of this silence is, the narrative of this psalm alone cannot reassure us that the singing resumes and the instruments are taken up again, but the psalm which follows begins with these words: 'I thank you, Lord, with all my heart; you have heard the words of my mouth.' Comforted with these words we might have hope that there is indeed a new song somewhere on the horizon but we cannot escape the irony that these words about silence are expressed in a song.

Sometimes, the weight of grief or loss can take away our ability to speak or indeed sing. I have noticed that when I have been faced with my own grief over the loss of a loved one, I have found it impossible to sing. I cannot wrench praise from my broken heart. I can only keep silent. My voice is an expression of what is going on within. When I have tried to sing or speak my voice quakes, it is fragile, weak and trembling. I have often had to deal with and respond to the grief of others, and have done so over many years, but when it comes to my own grief I cannot say anything at all. I have to retreat into silence. When his brother died, the opera singer Thomas Quasthoff could not sing either. Upon medical examination it was clear there was nothing physically wrong with his voice, it was his heart that was broken. The voice is 'the mirror of the soul' he said.[6]

[6] Interview with Thomas Quasthoff, The *Guardian*, Tuesday 17 August 2021 by Stephen Moss. 'Three days after being told that my brother would not live longer than nine months I lost my voice,' he recalls. 'Doctors looked at my throat and said: "Everything is fine." But my heart was broken, and if the heart is broken ...' he pauses. 'The voice is the mirror of the soul.'

The Sound of Silence

There is one occasion in the church's year when silence becomes the focus of our public liturgies and a form of communal lament. Remembrance Sunday, kept both in our churches and in civic and community gatherings at local war memorials, has become an annual tradition which seems to gain increasing attention as time, like an ever-rolling stream, stretches out from the global conflicts it commemorates. At the heart of Remembrance Sunday is two minutes of silence at 11am, usually book ended by a lone trumpeter playing the Last Post and Reveille. The silence becomes the sacramental action, the offering of the liturgy, the place towards which the liturgy gathers everyone together and the place from which the community are somehow commissioned to live out the words 'never again'. That silence carries many griefs which are beyond words and cannot even be spoken of. It carries many horrors which most of us cannot even comprehend, but we enter the darkness of this silence, touching the void of abject human folly and violence which results in despair, destruction, and death. How fragile that silence is and how powerful. What do you say in the face of such terror and such sadness experienced by so many? You say nothing and keep silent and hope that from this silence, peace can come. This form of silence, right at the heart of our civic religion is both horrific and salvific.

The formalised, corporate silence of Remembrance Sunday services and commemorations was something that the last surviving combat soldier of World War I could not face for most of his life. Harry Patch died aged 111 on 25 July 2009. At Paschendale, he witnessed the bloodshed, the dankness, the mud, lice and rats. He witnessed carnage on an industrial scale and like many veterans Harry never spoke of his experiences, he buried them. On Remembrance Sunday he religiously stayed at home, alone, and remembered. The painting *Two Minutes Silence* by Charles Spencelayh (1928) depicts an elderly man with head bowed. He is also at home, standing beside a table, his slippers beneath it, his reading glasses upon it. On a clock beside him, the time is shown as around eleven. There is a picture of his son, a soldier lost in the war, hung upon the wall. This is a representation of how many veterans and grieving families expressed their two minutes silence on Armistice Day, and among them Harry Patch. Two minutes of silence in an ocean of silence, repressing memories in almost unreachable depths. But as he approached his one hundredth birthday, Harry's subconscious began to agitate and his dreams became vivid and horrible. He could hold his silence no longer, the memories were bubbling up to the surface. It was time to wake up. The trumpet had sounded.

In the last few years of his life, and from his silence, Harry articulated a continued hope for peace in the world. He spoke of the stark and shocking realities of war that haunted him. He was brutally honest and honestly critical. His experience had turned him into a strident peacemaker and activist. At last, he had found his voice, and his voice needed to be heard and, given his age, with some urgency. He gave interviews on television and radio; he co-authored a book. Poems and rock songs were written about him, buildings and trains were named after him. He spoke at festivals. He met with an old enemy, who fought opposite him, Charles Kuentz was the only living German veteran at the time and they exchanged conversation and gifts: German butter biscuits for cider from Somerset. Harry finally laid a wreath at the Cenotaph. From his silence, Harry yearned for peace. He was eager for peace. He was angry for peace and he became very loud about it.

At the heart of every act of remembrance is the sound of silence. In that sacramental silence we honour the war dead of every generation. We also honour those who could not and cannot speak of what they witnessed in war. The shell shocked, the traumatized, the injured. We honour those whose voices were prematurely lost, those whose memories were buried deep in the dark cold earth, those who grieved through the night with little hope of joy coming in the morning. Silence can be a place of isolation and atomisation. It can be aggressive, growing secretly like cancer as Simon and Garfunkel sang, overwhelming life itself. Silence can hold its own counsel and say nothing in the face of evil and yet the sound of sheer silence can be the place where God is found.

The silence we make on Remembrance Sunday, is not for glory. In the silence, you don't hear a shell fired, you hear no explosion or cry of terror, you hear no empty words of consolation. There is no meaningless pomp and ceremony, no theatre, no politics, but you sense a deep and aching loss, an unending sorrow. From that same silence we also sense the first glimmers of hope for a future where swords will be beaten into ploughshares and spears into pruning hooks. The bugle stirs us to wake up, traditionally signalling the start of a new day as the sun rises in the sky, the emergence from silence calls us to live differently. As Maya Angelou suggests in her poem 'Amazing Peace', we hear the sound of peace emerging from violence, silencing war and hatred. Silence can be the place from which peace can emerge and hope can spring, it can be a place for prayer and pre-emptive of joy; it can make music and shape space, it is the place from which we become.

Silence leading to Song

There is a slither of a possibility that the prophet Ezekiel may have been one of those same exiles who sat down and wept by the rivers of Babylon. He is described as a priest, and was likely a priest of Jerusalem, holy and devout. His life would have revolved around the temple, its worship, and its sacrifices, for this was the place where the presence of God was to be found. The events surrounding the fall of Jerusalem and the violent enslavement and exile of the

Israelites ripped Ezekiel from the life of the temple and forced him to question whether God could be present with the faithful beyond the temple walls.

It was by the Babylonian River, Chebar, that Ezekiel received his extraordinary psychedelic vision of wheels and flashes of lightning and living creatures with wings. The vision was noisy and is described as being like the sound of floodwaters, like the sound of a storm, like the sound of an armed camp. And from this noise there came a voice. The voice commissions Ezekiel to be its mouthpiece, to speak to a rebellious people whether they hear or refuse to hear. To sweeten the task, Ezekiel is given a scroll to eat, a scroll containing lamentations, dirges, cries of woe and warnings, and yet the scroll tastes of honey, for a spoonful of sugar always makes the medicine go down more easily.

Of all the Hebrew prophets Ezekiel is one of the most extreme and in order to become the mouthpiece of God and carry God's voice- his own voice is silenced, his palate really is moulded to the top of his mouth and the only words he will be able to speak will be the words of God.[7] It is not such a leap of the imagination to consider that the loss of Ezekiel's voice was an expression of his grief. Because his lips are closed, his whole body becomes a mouthpiece which speaks through his demonstrative proclamations. His voice is made manifest in his physicality and in his silent protest. He lies on his left side for 390 days, he is confined in his own home, he pulls out his hair, he cooks bread on animal dung, he is unable to publicly mourn the death of his own wife and sing songs of lamentation. He is consumed by his grief and can only speak through silence.

At first, the way Ezekiel 'speaks' seems extreme to modern sensibilities, but there was something of an Ezekiel moment made visible when, in the summer of 2021, a retired Church of England Priest, Tim Hewes, literally, sewed up

[7]   Ezekiel 3:26.

his mouth in protest at the denial of the climate emergency. Before Reverend Hewes sewed up his mouth live to camera (by his own hand and with surgical thread), he said: 'Today there are countless people throughout the world who are voiceless and suffering because of the climate emergency. Climate science and truth has been muted, and those who suffer are not being heard.'[8] He said he had tried every other way to voice his concerns, but his voice was never heard, his words were not enough, so he sewed up his lips to make visible and demonstrate the warning he was being given to share – he was grieving for a dying world. The shocking video showing this seemingly mild-mannered vicar sewing up his lips in protest is gruelling to watch but the extremism of this action gave him and the millions affected by climate change the voice for which they longed and was heard loud and clear, albeit transiently in the daily news bulletins. It is one of the deepest ironies that sometimes silencing yourself gives you the loudest voice.

Silent protest, forsaking the voice to gain a voice, has long been a powerful means of enabling the voiceless to speak in the only way that is left open to them. This kind of silence is electric with the hope of justice. It is the kind of silence that is defiant and courageous. On 28 July 1917, more than ten thousand African Americans marched in silence down Fifth Avenue in what came to be known as the 'Silent Protest Parade'.[9] The march was in protest at the growing

---

[8]   https://www.facebook.com/ExtinctionRebellion/videos/breaking-revd-tim-hewes-71-has-sewn-his-lips-shut-outside-news-corp-offices-in-l/830497510929974/?extid=SEO----

[9]   The Conversation, 25 July 2017, Chad Williams, Associate Professor of African and Afro-American Studies, Brandeis University '100 years ago African-Americans marched down 5th Avenue to declare that black lives matter' https://theconversation.com/100-years-ago-african-americans-marched-down-5th-avenue-to-declare-that-black-lives-matter-81427

hatred and discrimination against African Americans and
the violence which had broken out a month earlier in East St
Louis, where white mobs shot, lynched, and stabbed anyone
who was black. In the Silent Parade in New York, women
and children dressed in white to symbolise the innocence
of the black community against the racism and violence
being inflicted upon them; men marched in dark suits with
banners declaring 'Thou shalt not kill'.

The only sound that could be heard was the beating
of drums as thousands marched in quiet dignity through
the city. The marchers remained absolutely silent. The co-
ordinator of the march was one James Weldon Johnson,
the first black leader of the National Association for the
Advancement of Coloured People (NAACP).[10] With the
support and assistance of local black clergy he mobilized the
community and led the march down Fifth Avenue. A flyer
sent out gave the reason for the parade: We march, it said,
because the growing consciousness and solidarity of race
coupled with sorrow and discrimination have made us one.
We march, it said, because we deem it a crime to be silent
in the face of such barbaric acts. James Weldon Johnson
had inaugurated that tradition of rising up against racism
and hatred which is seen again and again in the civil rights
protests of the 1960s and the Black Lives Matter marches and
protests of the early twentieth century. This silent protest
had given voice to those who were oppressed, victimised
and persecuted. It gave them a platform, a place from which
to 'speak', and offered hope in the face of despair.

James Weldon Johnson was also a writer and a poet
and used his beautiful literary voice to give hope to his
community. One of his gifts to those who were oppressed was
the poem 'Lift every voice and sing', which was set to music
by his brother John Rosamund Johnson. The Black National

[10]   https://beinecke.library.yale.edu/1917NAACPSilentProtestParade

Anthem, as it became known, articulated the hope that one day every voice will be heard between earth and heaven and justice and liberty will ring out for all. It imagined that one day there would be no need for silent protest because every person would be free to sing in their own God given voice. The song acknowledged the 'God of our silent tears' who was alongside the oppressed and the silenced as they sat down by the river and wept into their hands. This is the God who is there when we are at our lowest and most vulnerable ebb. This God enters into our vulnerability in Christ, who, with the beauty and music of his voice, becomes silent with us.

There is a sense that Jesus is silenced as he gets closer to the cross. As he walks the sorrowful way, paraded through the streets of the city, there is less he needs to say. When Jesus is brought before Pontius Pilate, he says very little, his words are becoming superfluous. It is his body which begins to speak. There is so much that Jesus could have said, there is so much that his voice could have wrought. Here is the voice which had already raised the dead, healed the sick, calmed the storm, turned water into wine; this is the voice that could make anything happen but in this moment this voice chooses to remain silent. Jesus says that everyone who belongs to the truth, will listen to his voice. Pilate asks, 'What is truth?' whilst failing to listen to the voice that was speaking the truth right in front of him. At this moment Jesus is the Good Shepherd, calling to the lost and drawing them to himself, protecting, shielding, guiding, and strengthening. Those who belong to the truth will hear this voice which does not speak, and to them it will speak volumes. Along with all those who have been silenced throughout history, Jesus says nothing. When Jesus stood before his accusers, he was silent, in this action he takes upon himself the cries of the silenced, all those who cannot speak are on his heart. He stands there like a lamb led to the slaughter, a silent sacrifice on behalf of the voiceless. As the prophet Isaiah says, he did not open his mouth.

Jesus' painful parade, carrying his cross, is a kind of embodied silence. With every step, speech becomes more and more superfluous, words dry up and there is no longer anything to say. On the cross, as this body weakens through pain and exhaustion, Christ retreats into a dark silence, and as he breathes his last, the sky turns black, and the curtain of the temple is torn in two. Even God the Father cannot speak, his heart, like the temple stones is broken. One imagines at this moment, the earth itself stops singing. Like an impending thunderstorm, the air is thick and mysterious and empty. There is a shift in all soundings as Christ journeys quietly into the very depths of humanity and into the darkness of hell, into the stillness and silence of death.

But it seems that silence is not our full end. We are promised that we will hear again the voice of mirth and gladness, the voice of the bridegroom and the bride, the voices of those who sing as they bring thanks into the house of the Lord.[11] From the cross, Christ leaps into silence and stirs up Sheol, rousing the dead back to life like a loud trumpet. Christ journeys to the depth of Hades and takes music into this deathly stillness. Christ sings the song of life as death scurries about in the dirt trying to find its sting, dry bones start to rattle and rise up from the dust. Christ is there breaking open the tombs with a song, waking the silent dead from their slumber, breathing into them the life that will never die and lifting up their voices to sing for joy. In Christ, silence always leads us to song.

[11] Jeremiah and the return of the Exiles, Chapter 33:10-12, 'there shall be once more heard the voice of mirth, and gladness, the voice the bridegroom and the voice of the bride, the voices of those who sing as they bring thank offerings to the house of the Lord'.

CHAPTER TEN

Therefore the World Glorifies Thee

Rejoice, O earth, in glory,
revealing the splendour of your creation,
radiant in the brightness of your triumphant king!
Christ has conquered, now his life and glory fill you,
darkness vanishes forever!
The Exultet

W hy do humpback whales sing? This is a scientific mystery which has yet to be fully fathomed. During the Cold War of the early 1950s, Frank Watlington, a US Navy engineer, was based at a secret listening post near Bermuda. He was alert and ready to identify Russian Submarines with his navy-grade hydrophones which enabled him to record underwater sounds and unusual frequencies echoing under the ocean waves. Imagine his surprise when he heard something so beautiful as to be enchanting. The something he heard was melancholic, plaintive, and lyrical. It wasn't a Russian submarine. This sound was like a voice, almost like someone singing. This was not a man-made sound; this was the sound of a living thing. His instinct told him that this mysterious sound, this sonorous incantation, was coming from the humpback whale and this would later be confirmed in a ground-breaking study by biologists Roger Payne, Katharine Payne, and Scott McVay.[1]

[1] Roger S. Payne and Scott McVay, 'Songs of Humpback Whales: Humpbacks emit sounds in long, predictable patterns ranging over frequencies audible to humans.' *Science*, 13 Aug 1971, Vol 173, Issue 3997, pp. 585-59

These three Bio-acousticians also happened to be musicians, and when they heard the sound of the humpback whale, they could find no other word to describe it, than a 'song'.[2] Deeper analysis found that the whale song could be broken down into defined rhythms, and fixed patterns, themes and repeated motifs. In his reflections on these discoveries, the Philosopher, Charles Hartshorne, offered that the Humpback Whale may be 'far closer to man as musician than is anything else on this planet'.[3] This sound, this invisible noise emanating from one of the largest creatures on earth, was from then onwards described as 'whale song' and yet, from that day to this, the ultimate purpose of this song remains a mystery. It seems to be the question that science cannot answer with any certainty: Why do humpback whales sing?

The whales were vocalizing something but what were they trying to say and to whom? What form of communication was this if it was even communication at all? It was not clear that the songs were for reproductive purposes alone, even though it was only the males of the species that were singing. It was clear that a variety of songs were sung across the global population of whales and more recent research shows that these songs ripple through the oceans from north, south, east and west. The repertoire was shared but the songs seemed to be continuously re-generating and evolving and changing over time. It is as if the whales are constantly called to sing a new song. As science has still not been able to give a definitive explanation, can we offer

[2] 'The Song of the Humpback Whale' was an album released in 1970 by CRM Records and co-produced by Payne. It became the best-selling environmental album in history. The popularisation of whale song and the response it emoted helped the 'Save the Whale' campaign as part of the environment movement.
[3] Charles Hartshorne, *Born to Sing: An interpretation and world survey of Birdsong* (Indiana University Press, 1973).

an answer to the question as to why the humpback whale sings? Could this singing be quite simply, praise? The whale song could be heard and interpreted as an exhortation, a proclamation, and an outpouring of joy from the creatures of this earth in praise of the being who created them. Nature, in all its fullness, complexity and diversity, might have the capacity to resonate with a frequency of jubilation which is heard not only on earth but by the angels of heaven.

Bless ye the Lord

The Benedicite *(Benedicite, Omnia Opera Domini)* is a canticle of the church often sung at the service of Matins, or Morning Prayer, in the Anglican Choral Tradition. It is described as a *Song of Creation* and in the 1662 Book of Common Prayer the canticle begins 'O all ye Works of the Lord, bless ye the Lord: praise him, and magnify him for ever.' The Canticle calls upon living creatures of all kinds to offer praise: Fowls of the air, Beasts and Cattle, and all green things upon earth. Even the sun, the moon and the stars of heaven are encouraged to join in the chorus of praise. It is a poetic representation of life in all its fullness and abundance giving praise to God as a condition of its being. In the current climate, as the earth experiences the effects of mass human consumption and destruction to the point of exhaustion, it is probably a song of the church that needs to be sung and recited more frequently. It is not only human beings that sing. The whole creation sings with us, but often, we don't have ears to hear it. Our anthropocentric view of life on our planet precludes our ability to appreciate that we are just one of many voices created to join in the song of the earth.

On an early morning train to London in the late spring, I was unexpectedly confronted with life in all its fullness simply existing in a state of praise. It was one of those journeys where the train seemed to be going so fast that you felt the earth turning beneath you. I was hurtling through between the north and the south of England, thinking about the meeting I was going to and letting the high-speed train carry my thoughts to new places. There were long stretches of the track running through the hills, and the fields were basking in the early morning sunlight. The sky was shimmering, the scene was beatific. As I looked from the window, quite literally watching the world go by, I saw a flock of Canada geese in a field. Oblivious to my gaze they were simply living, hustling together, probably chattering; they were just doing their thing, they were just being. I could not hear them, but they were sounding. It was a split-second scene to which I was privy, a flash of something I could barely understand or articulate. I felt for just a moment that I had been given a creator's eye view; a tiny snapshot into the innocence and beauty of what it means to be alive, a small insight into the gift of creation which so often passes us by. In those micro-seconds, a word came to mind as I watched those geese, the word was *zōē*, ζωή, life itself. This is the Greek word used in the Gospel of John to describe the kind of life that Christ brings when he says, 'I have come so that they may have life, and have it in plenty'.[4] I need to admit here that my New Testament Greek was never very good, I pretty much flunked it. I am not an able scholar of ancient languages, but that is the word I heard in my head and in my heart. It seemed to come to me from beyond and I was momentarily overwhelmed. I wanted to weep, in fact tears did come and the lump in the throat, but this was not a sadness I was channelling, but rather some kind of profound joy, this felt like some kind of blessing, some kind of realisation that the earth was singing.

This joy is the life which is daily sustained by God the

4   John 10:10.

creator, this joy is the life that never dies, the life that surges through creation and through every living thing. This is life as pure energy, as breath, as gift; this is life as hope, this is life as resurrection. Perhaps this is the life we see when we let creation just be creation; when we live and let live and look upon the life of our planet in all its beauty and miracle and join in with its praises. Pseudo-Dionysius writes that 'all life and living movement comes from a Life which is above every life and is beyond the source of Life. For this life souls have their indestructibility, and everything living, being and plant, down to the last echo of life, has life.' [5] Perhaps the whale song and the bird song and the song of every living thing which has ever and will ever walk upon this earth, was an expression and a vocalization of this kind of life. Life itself. Life from God.

The Benedicite calls specifically upon the whales, amongst all kinds of other creatures, to bless and praise the Lord and magnify the Lord for ever. These words meditate upon creation and articulate life on earth as an opening praise and a final doxology. I like to think that the writer of the Benedicite knew that the whales were singing, even though their song would have been beyond the limits of human hearing. The whale, as a biblical creature, also has a starring role in the story of Jonah the Prophet. In this story written at least five hundred years before the birth of Christ, we learn that the whale is a creature with praise in its belly. In the second chapter of the book, we find Jonah ensconced in the stomach of a big fish. Jonah cried out to the Lord and the Lord heard his voice. He concludes that after being swallowed whole by the passing sea creature it is only right to offer a sacrifice of praise to the Lord while being

[5] Pseudo-Dionysius, The Divine Names, Chapter Six, Concerning 'Life', 856B, in The Complete Works, Classics of Western Spirituality (Paulist Press, 1987).

impounded in its stomach. At that moment, when Jonah's cries of despair turn into songs of praise and thanksgiving, the Lord speaks to the fish, and it immediately vomits Jonah onto the dry land. The praise of God brings about liberation and forgiveness and Jonah is literally born again, spewed out like a baby being urged forth from the womb, or like new life emerging from a watery tomb, new worlds are begun, and praise is there at the moment of his re-birth.

We know it is not only the whales who sing. In one of those remarkable quirks of nature, it has been noted that, if you speed up the song of a humpback whale, to human ears at least, it takes on the sound of the likeness of a nightingale. O ye fowls of the air, bless ye the Lord: praise him, and magnify him for ever, rings out the Benedicite. If you are awake at about three or four o'clock on a spring morning you will hear the outpouring of praise by the birds of the air at the beginning of a new day. The cock crows. Blackbirds, Robins, Chaffinch all begin their individual offerings of praise as the light rises in the East. Birdsong is, strangely perhaps given their scale, a close relation to the song of the humpback whale in that there is rhythm, meter, themes, phrases and identifying features which relate to different populations and species. Again, this is described scientifically as a form of vocalization most usually theorised as relating to mating rituals or the marking of territory, but that never seems to be a completely satisfactory answer to the question: why do birds sing? It doesn't seem to do justice to the beauty of it all.

In many scientific studies there is always a remaining question as to *why*? Why is it that all sparrows sing the same song? Are these songs learnt or are they innate? Are these little birds given a song to sing before they even hatch from the egg? Before their feathers are formed and before they open their eyes is their song already laid down for all time in their tiny fluttering heart? Science can tell us many things, but it can never suppress the questions that relate to our being, purpose, and vocation. In the depths of winter, as day turns to dusk and the lights of evening shine around us, the starlings gather in murmuration, humming as they sweep through big skies. They fly in community soaring and swerving, making shapes in the moving air which look like a cloud, a bird, a heart, a wave. They give thanks and praise with one united voice to the God who made them, a song for eventide.

Bird Song

Olivier Messiaen (1908-1992) was an extraordinary composer whose deep Catholic faith and spirituality influenced all his works both sacred and secular. He was also enchanted and enraptured by the natural world and how it spoke (or sung) of God. Messiaen described himself as both an ornithologist and a theologian, and expressed his understanding of God through his music; he was particularly drawn to the meaning and message of birdsong as both a manifestation of God's love as expressed in and through nature, and also the praise that creation offers the Creator.[6] He transcribed birdsong into music,[7] the clarinet might sing the song of a blackbird and the violin sounded the nightingale, both birds that sing with the breaking of dawn.[8] It was as if he was trying to capture something of the praises of nature so that they could be articulated through human art. Perhaps he thought of this as a means of learning and educating ourselves in the art of the most authentic, unaffected, and heartfelt praise expressed by a living creature.

[6] *Messiaen's Language of Mystical Love*, edited by Siglind Bruhn from *The Introduction* by Siglind Bruhn (Routledge, 2012), p. 7.

[7] 'Réveil des oiseaux' (1953), 'Catalogue d'oiseaux' (1958) 'Oiseaux exotiques' (1956), are three of Messiaen's works where birdsong is used as a basis and theme of the composition.

[8] Richard Taruskin, 'Music in the Early Twentieth Century', *The Oxford History of Western Music* (Oxford, 2010), p. 239.

On Voice

It is hard to hear the singing of a blackbird and align the beauty of that song with the hostility of protecting a territory, or with the sole purpose of attracting a mate. It is much easier to imagine and even understand this song, as Messiaen did: poetically, and as an expression of identity, being and purpose, an aural assertion of a privileged place in God's creation. The singing of the creatures of this earth, whether whale or bird does not always have to be viewed as a purely utilitarian expression of biological want or need. There is a whisper of a possibility that the essence of these songs is for joy alone and an expression of being. There is even a chance that such songs might be sung not only by birds and whales, but by creatures of every kind, purely as an offering of praise, a subconscious expression of thanksgiving and love of life itself. This song could be an expression of a desire to pour out the self in offering to another in love, in a sacrifice of praise.

This is certainly the purpose and the end to which St Francis of Assisi believed all living things upon this earth were destined. In his *Laudes Creaturarum (the praises of the creatures),* known as the *Canticle of the Sun,* written in around 1224, he rejoices that everything, with every ounce of its breath, and with every particle of its being, is called to give praise and blessing to God. The sun, the moon and the stars resound with praise, every creature sings, every atom resonates with gladness. The earth is a ball of praise which sings unceasingly. Legend accords St Francis with preaching to the birds, and in his account, Brother Ugolino recalls St Francis' command to the birds to never neglect the study of praise. St Francis said that his 'little sisters' the birds, owing so much to the creator, were to always sing praise to God. [9]

[9]   *The Little Flowers of St Francis of Assisi,* Chapter XVI, Christian Classics Ethereal Library. This book of legends and stories associated with St Francis is attributed to Brother Ugolino Brunforte (1262-1348).

In his sermon, St Francis makes references to Matthew, chapter 6, where Jesus advises his disciples to look up at the birds of the air who are simply called to be as they were created, without concern for the body, or how the body is fed or adorned. Their only concern was their primary purpose, which was to offer praise, neither toiling nor spinning nor gathering into barns. These little birds were pure existence, totally resounding. As the disciples looked up, they heard the birds of the air making their song of praise, a song without words, without desire or design which made sense of everything as they walked through the dusty countryside around Jerusalem. When Jesus says, 'look at the birds of the air', and 'look at the lilies of the field' he points to them as examples of a life lived in praise. As the disciples looked upon the birds of the air and the lilies of the field, they might have seen them as I saw those geese from the window of a fast-moving train. We were looking on from a distance in silent wonder as the beautiful creatures of this earth offered silent praise to the Almighty, thereby drawing all of us into a state of praise with them.

Søren Kierkegaard reflected on the same passage from the Gospel of Matthew, and from a poet's eye view he imagined what it would be like to *be* a bird of the air or a lily of the field. [10] How wonderful it would be to be focused and tuned-in to nothing but God. How we might sometimes wish to escape our humanity and become like the birds of the air, so that we might move beyond our daily worries and anxieties and fly far, far away to greater things. [11] Kierkegaard takes us further beyond obvious praise and into silent praise, or even silent music. For he seems to be

[10]   Søren Kierkegaard, *The Lily Of The Field and the Birds of the Air: Three Godly Discourses*. Translated by Bruce H. Kirmmse, Princeton University Press (2016).
[11]   Psalm 55, verse 6.

suggesting that before the living God our voice falls mute as we slip more deeply into prayer, until we say nothing at all and simply bathe in God's presence. This, he says, is what the birds of the air and the lilies of the field can teach us. They teach us how to resound with praise and prayer without saying a single word. We are being directed to express ourselves with a voice which does not even require speech, the voice of our very being.

Resound with joy

From the smallness and the perfection of a bird, we can venture further into the essence of life as we now know it. If the trees, and the insects, and the waters are urged to offer praise then everything that combines to make the trees and the insects, and the waters must also be tuned for praise and inhabit the frequency of life. It turns out that all things, whether conscious or unconscious, are vibrating and there is a tendency for these vibrations to be shared or synchronised, across living things. In the Benedicite, less tangible things are also drawn into this hymn of blessing: clouds, fire, heat, winds, frost, cold, and lightnings. Even the things we cannot always see or touch are called upon as works of the Lord. With our twenty-first century ability to see beyond the tangible with the vision granted to us by magnetic resonance scanning, transmission electron microscopy and space telescopes, we can now peer even further into creation. And what do we find when we so peer? We find that even the DNA helix, the backbone of biological life oscillates and vibrates.[12] We find that the atom and the electron resonate in excitement, we find that our world, and everything within it, all that is seen and all that is unseen,

[12]   Chou K. C. (1984). Low-frequency vibrations of DNA molecules. *The Biochemical journal, 221*(1), 27–31. https://doi.org/10.1042/bj2210027

echo and resound with what we might decide to call praise. We are a musical instrument of epic proportions, a choir of frequencies and tones and timbres that together make one glorious sound.

If we peer at ourselves from the vantage of space, we come to understand that the earth itself, our blue planet, is humming and buzzing with life, micro-oscillating, resounding. If we look out into the universe, we see it shimmer and sparkle and we catch the echoes of its song coming to us across the chasm of millions of light years. It seems that the world and everything within it, and all things beyond it, resonates, praises, glorifies as one.

In 1977, two robotic Voyager probes were sent into interstellar space by NASA, where they remain to this day. With each probe was also sent a 12-inch golden phonograph record, containing a message from the whole of humanity to the waiting universe, and to unknown beings in as yet undiscovered worlds. These 'Sounds of the Earth' were catalogued by the astronomer, Carl Sagan, and sent into space with the Voyager Missions. In a billion years from now, when our earth is a bright star and we are all gone, the Golden Record might remain floating through space. If it was ever discovered, and if there were ever ears to hear it, they would receive words of greeting in 55 different languages by 55 different voices. They would hear the sound of humpback whales, birds singing, crickets clicking and frogs croaking. They would hear the sound of chimpanzees, the beat of a human heart, and the echo of laughter. They would also hear the songs of Aboriginal people, Indian raga, chants by the Navajo Indians alongside the music of J. S. Bach, Beethoven, Mozart's Aria, 'Queen of the Night' from the Magic Flute, and 'Johnny B. Goode' by Chuck Berry. If the Golden Record should ever be found, it would give a sound of the likeness of the voice of the earth.

At the end of all things, there will be a total consummation of all praise and perhaps this end is the direction towards which we all journey. This vision, this song, this 'Symphony of the Blessed' as Hildegard called it, is the purpose for which we were all created; the praise of God. All things in all places are drawn to this music, we are beckoned towards God, the Light of lights, and Sound of sounds, through whom all things were made. This God gathers all things to Godself, just as a hen tenderly gathers her chicks under the protection of her wings. Song after song is poured forth, and the songs are both an offering of perpetual praise but also a lament and a means of gathering every lost sheep back into the fold, each song a tributary of the crystal river. This one song will be so powerful it can call to repentance, it can heal, it can renew.[13]

There is no other purpose than to praise God with our lips, and in our heart and in our lives. Teilhard de Chardin, in his *Hymn of the Universe*, describes Christ as the principle of unity which saves our guilty world and its slow return to dust. It is, he says, through the force of his magnetism, the light of his teaching, and the unifying power of his very being; that Christ manifests at the heart of the world itself, the harmony of all endeavours and the convergence of all beings.[14] At the sound of Christ's voice there is a trembling and turbulence, there is a reshuffling of atoms and electrons and there is the bubbling up of praise from everything that has been made. The power of Christ through the resurrection will enliven all creation to sing, and ultimately save us from the dust. Christ is re-enchanting the world. He is teaching the world to sing. At his voice the creatures and created things of this earth cry out in glory and honour, at his voice the stars in

---

[13] Hildegard of Bingen, Book Three, Vision Thirteen, p. 533.
[14] Pierre Teilhard de Chardin, *Hymn of the Universe*, 74 (Collins, 1961), p. 147.

the heavens tremble with joy, every corner of the universe reverberates in exaltation.

The call of the church is to sing along with the voice of Christ in creation, a voice that can never be silenced. Even in the face of despair and darkness we are called to sing, even in the face of a future we cannot grasp we are to sing, even when faced with death, we are to sing, and even when we are stood weeping at the grave we make our song, 'Alleluia'.[15] At the end of all things, when all our earthly life is spent, we are still called to only one purpose. When all is revealed, when the end has come, we are called to only one purpose. On the last day we will sing. In the final text of our holy book, St John the Divine gives us a vision of eternity, and the only activity of this eternity is song. Everything is song. Everything is praise. Everything is drawn to this one purpose: to sing. And at the heart of the song is a voice, which speaks from the throne of God.

Exult all creation

On the Eve of Easter, in a darkened church, a small fire is lit at the porch. Bodies gather, faces are bathed in light. Fire is primal, and in the gloom it makes the heart bright. The flames take us to our beginnings and our endings, the flames draw us in and offer warmth and comfort, and we know that from fire, voices can come. From the fire a candle is lit, it is the paschal candle which shines with a light that no darkness can quench. Into the darkness of the church, the candle is carried, step by step, a single source of light piercing the shadows. Flame flickering, the bodies follow, and a voice sings 'The Light of Christ', and all respond 'Thanks be to God'. This is sound and light entwined, as it

[15]   'Dust thou art and unto dust shalt thou return.'
All we go down to the dust; and weeping o'er the grave
we make our song: Alleluia, alleluia, alleluia.
The Russian Contakion of the Departed

was at the beginning of all things, this is a new creation. The candle and the voice stop, and under the light of the candle the voice sings again. This time the voice sings one of the most beautiful songs of the church, a hymn of profundity and praise, only sung on this specific day at this specific time, marking Jesus' return from the depths of hell, bringing the universe back to life.

The song is called the *Exultet*. This hymn is properly sung by a Deacon, a minister called to be the servant of all; a minister who, in the liturgies of the church always stands at the door and on the threshold between worlds, a voice from the world into the church and a voice from the church into the world. At the end of the Eucharist, it is the Deacon's voice that dismisses the gathered assembly and sends them out into the world to love and serve the Lord. On Easter Eve, it is the Deacon who is called to sing the great Exultet. This time they stand at the threshold of heaven and earth, at the threshold of life and death. They sing the song which resounds with the good news of the resurrection, calling the whole world, the universal church, and the universe itself to rejoice with the whole company of heaven. This is part of the great song of praise that God has created to sound through all eternity and 'those who enter the community of God join this song.'[16] Dietrich Bonhoeffer in *Life Together* describes the song of the resurrection as the song of the morning stars as God created the world. This is the great song of praise

[16]   'God has prepared for Himself one great song of praise throughout eternity, and those who enter the community of God join in this song. It is the song that the "morning stars sang together and all the sons of God shouted for joy" at the creation of the world. (Job 38:7). It is the victory song of the children of Israel after passing through the Red Sea, the Magnificat of Mary after the annunciation, the song of Paul and Silas in the night of prison, the song of the singers on the sea of glass after their rescue, the "song of Moses the servant of God, and the song of the Lamb" (Rev. 15:3) It is the song of the heavenly fellowship.' Dietrich Bonhoeffer, *Life Together*.

that was sung as the waters of the red sea parted and the people of Israel crossed onto dry land. This is the song of Mary after the angels' visitation, the song of Paul and Silas in their imprisonment, the song of Moses and the lamb. This is the song that is sung in the midst of grief and in places of darkness and fear, it is the song that gives courage to the fearful, hope to the lost and a voice to those who have been silenced for too long. In the life of the church, the Exultet makes manifest this song on the most holy night of the year when hell is vanquished and death is defeated.

In the darkness of a church this song is sung by the light of a single candle made from the wax of bees who sang as they worked. When this song is sung, all things are made again. Of all the songs I have ever sung, this is the song which feels like it is carving out a new world, it feels as if all things are being made new, it feels like you are conducting an immense gathering, the church on earth and the church in heaven join forces through your voice, the song is being sung in and through you. This is a song of invocation, a song of courage and hope, a song of healing and cleansing, this is a song that calls upon the universe to come together and offer praise; it calls upon the earth and the splendour of all creation to rejoice as one. This song calls us back to our beginning and back to our first vocation. This song calls upon each one of us, and every corner of the universe to resound in praise, and in this song, all voices find their purpose.